MW00805244

TRUST & CONFIDENCE

INSIDE THE BATTLE BETWEEN THE
SECRET SERVICE AND KEN STARR

Donna & Tom —
Thanks For your Support

ISBN: 979-8-218-22298-7
First Edition: September 2023

10 9 8 7 6 5 4 3 2 1

Excerpts from The Secret Service by Philip H Melanson, copyright © 2002. Reprinted by permission of Basic Books, an imprint of Hachette Book Group, Inc.
Front cover dust jacket image copyright © 2023 Getty Images, Photograph by Dirck Halstead.

Library of Congress Control Number: 2023941269

TRUST & CONFIDENCE

INSIDE THE BATTLE BETWEEN THE
SECRET SERVICE AND KEN STARR

BY

JIM LICHTMAN

Scribbler's Ink Press

*"If you have integrity, nothing else matters.
If you don't have integrity, nothing else matters."*

—Senator Alan Simpson

Prologue

Five minutes into my interview with Lewis Merletti, the former director of the United States Secret Service looked me in the eye and said unequivocally, "The way I'm going to tell you this is *exactly* the way it happened."

In 1998, for the first time in our nation's history, the director of the United States Secret Service was asked to testify against a sitting president. Independent counsel Kenneth W. Starr wanted to question Director Merletti about President William Jefferson Clinton's relationship with White House intern Monica Lewinsky.

Based on alleged inside information, Starr issued a motion to compel Merletti and agents protecting the president to testify as to what they may have seen or heard regarding Clinton's intimate liaisons with Lewinsky.

In a declaration made in opposition to the motion, Merletti argued that if agents were permitted to testify about anything other than criminal acts, it would compromise the *trust and confidence* tenet critical to the mission of the Secret Service and thus jeopardize the safety of the presidency and the country.

"BEING WORTHY OF TRUST AND CONFIDENCE," the declaration states, "is the absolute heart and soul of the United States Secret Service. This trust and confidence cannot be situational. It cannot have an expiration date. And it must never be compromised."

With the support of all living former directors, the upper echelon of the Department of Justice (DOJ), the US solicitor general, and former president George H. W. Bush, Merletti battled the independent counsel for six months, taking his case all the way to the Supreme Court.

Even after the legal fireworks ended and Merletti had retired, one inexplicable twist remained to test the former director's fortitude.

At the end of our first interview, which would become a series, little did I know that this would be the beginning of extensive research that would cover twelve years. That initial meeting led me to review documents from Merletti's personal files as director; to speak to the special counsel charged with investigating claims of misconduct by the Office of Independent Counsel; to search for her report, which she was led to believe had been sealed by the court; to speak to several former Starr prosecutors; and to spend nine years searching DOJ and the Starr/Ray/Thomas independent counsel files in the National Archives.

During that time, I would not only be the first to uncover special counsel Jo Ann Harris's investigation into the "brace" (confront for questioning) of Monica S. Lewinsky but would also locate a letter from Starr's source inside the Secret Service signed "Deep Throat," the pornographic metaphor that became synonymous with the secret source of information in Nixon's Watergate scandal. Starr's Deep Throat, however, was wholly false, part of one individual's plan to discredit

Merletti by alleging a deal between the director and President Clinton: in exchange for his silence on Lewinsky, Clinton would appoint Merletti Secret Service director.

As I left Merletti's office, I realized I had possibly come across a story of integrity unlike anything I had ever heard before—one that would pit two factions of the Justice Department against one another: Starr's Office of Independent Counsel and the upper echelon of the department that supported Merletti's argument.

This is about a fight between reason and rationalization, between moral integrity and moralistic righteousness. It's a battle between one man standing on principle and another who believed the end justified the means.

1

On March 30, 2000, former US Secret Service Director Lewis Merletti was preparing to speak to an audience of FBI agents at their National Academy on Ethics and Leadership in Cleveland, Ohio. He was invited to speak about the character traits necessary for leadership. He was also there to share his experience with Whitewater independent counsel Kenneth Starr, which consumed much of his time as Secret Service director in 1998.

Walking backstage, two agents approached Merletti.

"We wanted to be the first to meet you, sir," one agent said, extending his hand.

"A great pleasure," the second agent added. "What will you be speaking on today?"

"I'm going to talk about ethics, leadership, and integrity, and I'll be speaking a bit about Ken Starr," Merletti replied.

Starr had occupied the morning slot at the conference. After learning this, Merletti asked for equal time in the afternoon.

"Man, he sure did a *great* job this morning!" the first agent said.

Always low-key, Merletti said, "Well, I'll have some things to say that may not be quite so positive."

The second agent looked the former director squarely in the eyes. "Sir . . . I hope you're wearing a bulletproof vest today."

"I'm just here to tell the truth," Merletti said.

The Whitewater scandal has its genesis in a *New York Times* story published during the 1992 presidential election revealing that Bill and Hillary Clinton had lost money in a failed real estate project known as the Whitewater Development Corporation in Arkansas, where Bill Clinton was governor.

The story caught the attention of Resolution Trust Corporation (RTC) investigator, L. Jean Lewis, who was examining the failure of Madison Guaranty, an Arkansas-based savings and loan owned by Jim and Susan McDougal. The closer Lewis looked, the more troubling connections she found between the McDougals, the Clintons, and Madison. After several criminal referrals by RTC to the Department of Justice, Clinton, now president, asked Janet Reno, attorney general, to open an investigation to quickly put the issue behind him. Reno then appointed veteran federal prosecutor and Republican Robert B. Fiske, Jr. as the regulatory independent counsel to investigate the matter.

When the Independent Counsel Statute was renewed by Congress, Fiske, despite years of experience, was replaced by Kenneth W. Starr, a judge with *no* experience as a federal prosecutor, by a three-judge panel known as the Special Division of the Court of Appeals for the District of Columbia. The judges were selected by William H. Rehnquist, Chief Justice of the United States Supreme Court.

A similar incident occurred in 2020 when attorney general William P. Barr removed Geoffrey S. Berman, the US attorney for the Southern District of New York, a prosecutor with years of experience, and replaced him with US Securities and Exchange Commission chairman Walter Joseph "Jay" Clayton, a man with no experience as a federal prosecutor. Both actions strongly suggested political intentions.

To fully understand why Starr was so interested in the Secret Service, it's necessary to examine the context of the independent counsel office in early January 1998.

After a nineteen-month Freedom of Information Act (FOIA) request, I obtained a copy of a one-hundred-page report detailing a special counsel investigation conducted by former Department of Justice assistant attorney general for the Criminal Division Jo Ann Harris and her co-counsel, Mary Francis Harkenrider. The two attorneys were brought in by Robert W. Ray who took over for Ken Starr in the fall of 1999 after Starr returned to private practice. Harris and Harkenrider's job was to investigate allegations of professional misconduct by OIC in its treatment of Monica Lewinsky at the Ritz-Carlton Hotel on January 16, 1998.

According to the report, after reaching dead ends in Whitewater, Filegate, Travelgate, and the death of deputy White House counsel Vince Foster, OIC was in the process of winding down its investigation when it received a late-night phone call from Linda R. Tripp. Speaking to Starr's deputy, Jackie Bennett, Tripp revealed that her Pentagon coworker, Monica Lewinsky, had been intimately involved with the president. Conversations secretly recorded by Tripp supported her account.

Before her death in 2014, Harris told me, "When Tripp made that phone call to the Washington office, the whole place just *lit up*. It just rescued their investigation."

With Tripp's revelations about the president's relationship with Lewinsky, along with a tip from a covert source inside the Secret Service, Starr's prosecutors focused with bulldog obsession on getting Merletti to confess to an alleged deal he made with Clinton: keep quiet about Lewinsky, and I'll make you the next director.

Six months after Clinton was sworn in for a second term, Lewis C. Merletti became the nineteenth director of the Secret Service. Starr and his deputies were convinced that this fact, along with others, confirmed their source. In an interview, Merletti says he never asked for the job. As he described, he was one of several candidates recommended for the post. It was only after many rounds of interviews that he was chosen as the new director and sworn in on June 6, 1998, by Treasury Secretary Robert E. Rubin.

This was not the first time I had spoken with Merletti. In 1999, I interviewed him for my book *What Do You Stand For?* The book was an anthology of responses from more than a hundred individuals to a questionnaire: *What do you stand for? What principles have you lived by? Describe a moment of principle when your convictions were tested.*

His response revealed his approach to leadership, the importance of the mission, and a passionate defense of that essential tenet of all ethical values, integrity.

"My life lessons go back to 1967 with my enlistment in the United States Army," Merletti wrote. "At the age of nineteen, I completed basic training, advanced infantry training, and jump school. I was recruited into the US Army's Special Forces Training Group. There, I completed one year of Special Forces qualification courses, then on to Vietnamese language school.

"During my tour of duty in Vietnam, I learned many things. It was my first exposure to leading people in a stressful, often hostile environment. I experienced cultural diversity. Our Special Forces team consisted of whites, blacks, Hispanics, and American Indians. We depended on each other; we trusted each other; we cared about each other; we were a *team*. We worked alongside the Montagnards, Cambodians, and Vietnamese, and we were a team. We lived their culture and learned not to impose ours upon them. We were accepted by them, and our mission succeeded."

"Those lessons," Merletti said, "became the foundation for the principles that guided me throughout my career in the United States Secret Service, an agency composed of highly dedicated men and women."

"As I rose through the ranks, ultimately becoming the nineteenth director of the United States Secret Service (USSS), I developed a reputation of team building, vision, and forward-thinking. I earned the respect of those who worked for me because I took the time to understand what they do. I worked at creating an atmosphere to encourage innovation, creativity, and a sense of purpose. As director, I reinforced our oath of commitment and accountability to the 269 million people of the United States of America. As an agency, we stood united against the likes of Ramzi Yousef and Timothy McVeigh."

"During my tenure as director," Merletti said, "the Secret Service experienced one of its most critical tests. That test came in the form of the Office of Independent Counsel's request for Secret Service testimony. Never in the history of our agency had we been asked to violate our standard of trust and confidence.

"Members of USSS inherited a long-lasting institutional culture; a tradition that centers on dedication; and an ethic centering on a sense of duty, honor, and love of country. A career in the Secret Service is more than a 'job'; it is a commitment to the American way of life.

"The decision I made, however, was not made in a vacuum. Although I had a strong sense of what the Service's position should be, I sought the counsel of all four living former directors. When I asked what they would do, to a man they answered, 'Trust and confidentiality *is* what this agency has always stood for. You're the first to be tested. Don't let us down.'"

What critical test was Merletti talking about? Why was he being asked by the independent counsel to violate an agency standard, and what decision did he make that called for the involvement of four former directors?

For much of 1998, I was traveling around the country speaking to corporations, associations, and schools on the importance of ethics. Beyond a general familiarity with Starr's investigation of Clinton, I was unaware of how or why the Secret Service had become part of the story.

I followed up with Merletti for more details.

"I received your letter dated May 4, 1999, requesting additional information," he wrote back. "I would prefer not to go into any details regarding my experience with the independent counsel's office."

I'd barely finished reading that last sentence when I immediately thought, "My God, this guy has a story to tell."

I picked up the phone and called his office. His associate, Kat Mathis, put me through to the former director, now working as head of security for the Cleveland Browns.

"Hey, Jim, how are you?"

I explained that I wasn't aware of this critical test or exactly what decision he had to make, that I needed more details.

"Jim, this was the most painful period of my life, and I don't intend to go back over it."

That was followed by a long pause.

I couldn't think of anything else to say other than to quietly empathize. "It must've been difficult for you."

The floodgates opened.

"*Nobody* knows what it was like," Merletti began, and as he talked, I started taking notes.

"I called the four former heads of the Secret Service into my office and explained what Independent Counsel Starr wanted, that he wanted all agents on the president's protective detail to talk about what they may have seen or heard regarding the president's intimate relationship with Monica Lewinsky. The history of the Secret Service provides a strong foundation for this tradition of unequivocal trust. For the Secret Service, *trust and confidence* was decidedly nonpartisan and nonpolitical.

"We live according to an unwritten code," Merletti stressed, "an invisible web of obligation; we would sooner die than fail."

He paused for a moment before adding, "Is that what you're looking for?"

"*Yes,*" I said, trying to contain my surprise, wanting to know more.

The standard of *trust and confidence* became the central argument for Merletti's decision to challenge Starr's motion to compel agents' testimony regarding Bill Clinton's presidential life. This was the only time a Secret Service director was put to an extraordinary test of integrity where the Service was drawn into a deeply partisan issue. Although the battle between OIC and the Secret Service had been reported in news accounts, this inside detail was something I believed no one had heard before.

I finished writing this up and included his story in my book, believing that would be the end of it.

2

In the spring of 2007, I was speaking to a corporate group in Arizona. The speaker ahead of me was Frank Sesno, then Washington, DC, bureau chief at CNN. He complimented me on my ethics talk, and I used it as an opening.

"You know, Frank, CNN needs to do a special on ethics. It's an issue that's behind many of today's news stories."

Sesno agreed, adding, "We've discussed it but haven't come up with the right idea."

"Let me write something up and send it to you," I suggested.

About a week later, I sent Sesno a few pages describing three different stories. I chose the Merletti story because it involved a high-ranking government official who faced a painful ethical crisis.

Sesno liked what I showed him. "But if you're going to produce this," he said, "you'll have to interview these people first."

Once again, I called Kat Mathis, explained the project, and asked if Merletti would be willing to participate. He agreed.

"How much time would you need?" Mathis asked.

"An hour, hour and a half would be nice."

I arrived at Merletti's office and clipped microphones on both of us. He spoke for almost three hours. I had worked up eleven questions, but I only had to ask one: When did you first learn that Ken Starr wanted to question agents about President Clinton's involvement with Monica Lewinsky?

"Our chief counsel, John Kelleher," Merletti began, "informed me by phone that we would be getting subpoenas from the independent counsel for agents on the president's protective detail to testify."

As Merletti recalled, his reaction was immediate: "What is this guy *thinking*, John? Does he know what this means?"

"Look," Kelleher tried to assure him, "Ken Starr is a reasonable guy. I've worked with him before. Once we explain things to him, Lew, this will all be a nonissue."

At the independent counsel's offices on Pennsylvania Avenue, Merletti and Kelleher stood before Ken Starr and his deputy, Robert J. Bittman, as the Secret Service director laid out his reasoning why agents should not testify about the president's life by way of an extraordinary PowerPoint presentation detailing Secret Service history and its vital mission.

"An assassination has grave effects," Merletti emphasized. "It's not like any other murder. It's a murder that has worldwide implications. Secret Service history has proven that confidentiality affords us the proximity that is critical to the success of our mission. *Proximity*," Merletti stressed to Starr and Bittman, "is the difference between life and death to our protectees. If our protectees cannot trust us, if they believe that we will be called to testify before a grand jury to reveal confidences, the president will not allow us that critical proximity."

When the director finished, Starr responded, "Mr. Merletti, this office has the highest respect for the Secret Service and all that your agents do. Now," he said, looking at his notes, "I'd like your agents to tell me, when women came out of the Oval Office, did any of your agents observe that their lipstick wasn't on right or their hair was mussed? Did they ever hear any sounds?"

The Secret Service director was incredulous. "You *are* kidding?"

"No, sir, I am not," Starr said in the polite and courtly manner he was known for.

"You have no questions about the presentation?" Merletti asked.

"That's what I want to know. That, along with the postings of agents in and around the Oval Office."

"That's what I'm trying to avoid," Merletti said, "giving the specifics on where our agents are, how they do their job, because when you give that away, it's going to come out somewhere in newspapers or magazines. We're giving away our protective advantage. If you know where we are, you know how to defeat us."

"From the very beginning," Merletti told me, "Starr wasn't listening to what I had to say. He had been told by someone that the Secret Service was highly involved in a cover-up. It was obvious to me that he'd been fed this information, and he was naive enough to believe it, and it could not have been further from the truth."

Throughout the entire three hours, Merletti remained clear, focused, and persuasive as he related what happened in almost chronological order.

"I was fighting for two things," he explained. "Number one, I know that it's trust and confidence in us that allows us proximity to our protectees. And I know that our protection is like a science. You must have proximity because it's all about cover our protectee, the president, and evacuate him. By cover, we mean stepping in the line of fire, stepping in front of a bullet."

Merletti described special agent Tim McCarthy's immediate response to protect President Ronald Reagan during the 1981 attack by John Hinckley Jr. As McCarthy spread out and covered—stopping a bullet intended for Reagan—special agent Jerry Parr whisked the president into a car before it sped away. McCarthy was seriously wounded in the attack.

"I can't outrun a bullet," Merletti said. "None of us can. We have to have proximity. We can't do it from across the room. We can't do it with smoke and mirrors. And we train at it, and train at it, and train at it, so that we can immediately step in front of him."

Despite the detailed examples in the director's lengthy presentation, Starr remained unconvinced.

"He was on a mission," Merletti declared, "and I firmly believe that it was driven in large part by politics."

Starr then played his trump card.

"Someone at that meeting said, 'We have information that *you*, Mr. Merletti, were involved in putting the president in the back seat of a car, covering him with a blanket, taking him out of a White House context, getting Monica Lewinsky there, and allowing them to be alone in a room.'"

Merletti was stunned. "Who told you this?"

"Oh, I can't tell you that," Starr said.

"He had some type of information," Merletti said, "some 'Deep Throat' type of information, and he believed this information, and it could not have been further from the truth."

At this point, neither Merletti nor I were aware of a letter from a source inside the Secret Service buried in the independent counsel's files in the archives that I would later discover. The letter was signed "Deep Throat."

The name, of course, originates from *Washington Post* reporter Bob Woodward's covert Watergate source as detailed in Woodward and Carl Bernstein's 1974 book *All the President's Men*. Due to his access to high-level information in the executive branch, the source supplied information to steer the reporters' investigation. Later, Mark Felt, the number-two at the FBI at the time, came forward and identified himself as the source. (In re-examining Felt's information twenty years later, however, Woodward wrote, "Reviewing everything Felt said to me, it is apparent he was wrong on a number of things.") Nonetheless, after the release of the Robert Redford/Dustin Hoffman film in 1976, the perception of his significance only grew as the character became indelible in storied journalism and the public's mind.

Recalling his decision-making, Merletti said, "I not only had to be concerned about the Secret Service and President Clinton, but I had to be concerned about the Secret Service and every president that was to follow. Let me show you something," he said, reaching for a book on a table in front of us with stacks of files.

Truth at Any Cost, published in 2000 by reporters Susan Schmidt and Michael Weisskopf, was among the first books detailing Starr's investigation. Merletti opened the book and read a passage: "Starr's investigators spent weeks trying to corroborate Clinton's alleged Oval Office directive to Merletti."

"Now," Merletti said, "somewhere there's an allegation that I was told by the president that I wouldn't talk to anyone about Monica Lewinsky. That never happened, but there was an allegation."

Merletti pulled a bookmark and read another passage:

The tip came from a source connected to the Secret Service's top command. He told OIC that shortly after the New Year, Clinton had called Merletti into the Oval Office and given him marching orders: "I want Secret Service lawyers to research the question of executive privilege. I don't want anything coming out of the Secret Service about women."

"[Starr] spent hundreds and hundreds of man-hours," Merletti recounted, "trying to find out that this happened. Because when he asked me, I said, 'Wait a minute, I can tell you right now that *never* happened. I was never directed. I'm doing this because of the Secret Service. I'm doing this [keeping agents from testifying] on principle. I'm standing up for the integrity of the United States Secret Service.'

"He couldn't believe," Merletti reacted, anger building, "he *didn't* believe in integrity, which makes me think he had very little integrity, because he can't even recognize it when he sees it."

"How did he respond when you told him that it never happened?" I asked.

"It was like talking to a wall," Merletti said. "He would just go, 'OK, explain to me how your agents could have seen . . .' It was like he never, ever listened to me."

Merletti read another passage:

The normally placid Holder [Eric Holder, deputy attorney general to Janet Reno] was agitated. "Merletti's ready to go nuclear on you guys," he said. . . . He was prepared to call a press conference to blast Starr and the FBI, said Holder.

"That's putting it mildly," Merletti said, "and believe me, I'm a very low-key person." He read from another passage:

The Secret Service director had just learned that Starr's FBI agents had interviewed his predecessor, Eljay Bowron, without clearing the interview with him. . . . Starr had dispatched investigators to question Bowron about his resignation in 1997.

"My predecessor, Eljay Bowron," Merletti described, "was working somewhere in DC and lived in Virginia. Two FBI agents show up at his home, and his wife's there, alone.

"'Who's there?' Bowron's wife asks.

"'We're with the FBI.'

"'I'm not opening the door.'

"'We need to speak to your husband.'

"'He's not here.'

"'Well, where is he?'

"'He's at work.'

"'Well get him on his cell phone. We need to talk to him.'

"She would not let them in," Merletti said.

"Just to be clear," I interrupted, "these were FBI agents investigating for Starr, who had come to the home of the former director of the Secret Service, Eljay Bowron, and were speaking to his wife on the other side of the front door?"

"Correct. I just want to give you a taste of what we were up against. She calls Eljay, and he tells her that he is on the Metro [in DC] and will be getting off at the next stop in about ten to fifteen minutes. She tells the agents that he'll be home in about twenty minutes."

"Where is he?" the agent pressed. "We need to see him."

After learning which stop her husband was due to get off at, the agents drove over, met the former director, then ushered him into the back seat of their car. According to Merletti, their conversation went something like this:

"We're investigating for Starr," the first agent said. "We *know* what happened."

"What do you know happened?" Bowron asked.

"We know that Merletti cut a deal with President Clinton that he would become director and would remove you," the agent explained. "The president said, 'Don't talk about Monica Lewinsky. I'll get rid of Eljay and I'll make you the director.'"

"Well, that never happened," Bowron calmly said.

"How do you know?"

"Because I was the one who approached Merletti about being director, and he did not want to do it. In fact, he absolutely did not want to do it!"

Bowron believed Merletti had the essential leadership traits and pressed him to take the job. Ultimately, Merletti agreed to go through the selection process, along with fifteen other nominees. During his tenure as director, Merletti would frequently speak to the "formers," as he dubbed them.

"I realized that I was the caretaker in this position," Merletti continued. "It's about more than me; it's about the entire legacy of the

Secret Service. I interacted with Clint Hill [the agent on Kennedy's protective detail in Dallas], who had stayed away from the Secret Service for a long time. He's a hero of ours. I tried to glean as much information from all the 'formers' because I didn't want decisions made in a vacuum. I always want to hear from others.

"So now we're in the back seat of the FBI car with Bowron," Merletti resumed.

"'Merletti did this whole thing,' an agent pushed the former director. 'He's the one who orchestrated your being removed.'

"'No,' Bowron said. 'I know he didn't.'

"'You tell us that he did. You *know* he did!'

"'It didn't happen. I had to almost put him in a headlock to get him involved in it.'

"'Tell us the truth. He did this!'

"'*No!*'

"'You were *forced* out. You know you were!'

Finally, Bowron had enough. "Look, I gave you my answer. I answered you *three* times. You are not going to ask me that question again. You're taking me home, and I'm getting out of this car."

I told this story to former assistant attorney general Jo Ann Harris.

"Doesn't surprise me," Harris said. "That's a method the FBI has used before. In fact, they used it on a former federal judge in New York."

A short time later, Bowron phoned Merletti and described what happened. Angered, Merletti called Eric Holder late that same evening.

"Who do these FBI agents and Ken Starr think they are?" Merletti asked the deputy AG. "Do you think for a minute that if the Secret Service was involved in any investigation about the FBI that we wouldn't call the FBI and tell them that we were going to interview a former director of the FBI? Do you think we would be so disrespectful as to put him in the back seat of a car and treat him like he just robbed a bank and make allegations—'No you're not telling us the truth; we know what happened'?"

Merletti's voice began to rise. "I said, 'You need to get to Ken Starr and tell him this has got to stop. And let me tell you something, Eric, this is not the first thing. This is probably the *tenth* thing that's happened.'

"It was inappropriate, disrespectful, out of line," Merletti emphasized. "My point was, these guys, they're chasing shadows. There are terrorists in this country that are setting up to hit us, and *this* is what Ken Starr and the FBI are wasting time on? Someone gave Starr this information, and no matter what I did or what I said, he was on a mission to prove this stuff was true."

"So, it was Starr's contention that you were colluding with President Clinton on all this?"

"*Totally*," Merletti stressed. "Never, ever did President Clinton . . . I mean, the fact that he believed that the president would offer . . . 'I'll get rid of Eljay Bowron and make you the director.' It's childish, absolutely childish. In the Secret Service, we don't operate that way. In the White House, we don't operate that way."

This wasn't Merletti's first political rodeo, and he had the battle scars to prove it.

3

In 1995, Special Agent Lewis Merletti sat before a joint House subcommittee to respond to questions concerning a Treasury report he investigated and helped write regarding the siege on the Branch Davidian compound near Waco, Texas.

In 1993, the Branch, as it was called, was a religious sect led by spiritual zealot Vernon Wayne Howell, better known as David Koresh. The Bureau of Alcohol, Tobacco, and Firearms (ATF) had evidence the group had amassed a large collection of illegal weapons. After obtaining a search warrant for the compound and arrest warrants for Koresh and several other Branch members, ATF was attempting to serve the warrants when a fierce gun battle broke out between federal agents and sect members, resulting in the deaths of four ATF agents and six Davidians.

The FBI took charge, surrounding the compound for fifty-one days. After negotiations between Koresh and the FBI had collapsed, and concern for the safety of the children inside the compound had increased, the FBI, with the approval of Attorney General Reno, launched an assault on the compound, using vehicles to punch holes in the walls of the buildings and insert tear gas to safely force the occupants out of the structures. During the assault, a fire broke out and quickly consumed the compound, leading to the deaths of eighty Branch members, including Koresh.

In the immediate aftermath, the FBI was accused of having initiated the fire. However, evidence later showed that the fire began in three different locations inside the compound. Many of the deaths inside the buildings were determined to have been caused by "gunshot wounds apparently inflicted by fellow cult members," the report concluded.

While working with the Secret Service out of the Baltimore office, Merletti received a call from director John Magaw, who had been named as a replacement for the head of ATF.

"I'm transferring you out of Baltimore," Magaw told him. "You're coming back down here, but you're going to Treasury. You're going to head up the investigation for Waco."

"Now, I really didn't want to do that," Merletti said, "but it's not my choice. So I go down to Waco. I had a team of eighteen investigators. I selected some from Secret Service, Customs, IRS [Internal Revenue Service], from all different investigative agencies. I interviewed them all, and I selected them all. Assistant Secretary of the Treasury for Enforcement Ron Noble oversaw the investigation.

"We investigate the whole thing, and we realized that ATF made huge mistakes. The director of ATF had to leave. Several office people had to be fired. It wasn't a pleasant thing.

"We write a book, and it's about that thick," Merletti described, "and I had to testify in front of Congress. It was my first time testifying before Congress, and immediately, I'm attacked by these Republicans: 'So, you're Lew Merletti. You're the guy that orchestrated the cover-up!'

"*What?*" Merletti silently said to himself.

"Now, I'm being accused for the first time. This is in front of Congress; every newspaper in Washington is there."

The White House was concerned because they believed that congressional opponents "were trying to say that Janet Reno had messed up, that the secretary of the Treasury messed up, that the president was involved, that it was just a debacle," Merletti recalled. "There were mistakes made, but they were all made by ATF."

As the political rhetoric by committee members ramped up, Merletti began clenching his jaw.

"It took me a couple of minutes to realize what was going on. I had to wait until my time to speak, and then, I was very strong in my response."

On day two of the hearings, Merletti took exception to the previous day's testimony by an ATF supervisor who harshly criticized the report. In calm and clear language, Merletti voiced his objections.

"He's making accusations that this report was unfair, biased, and a cover-up. I stand behind the solid integrity of this report," Merletti told the subcommittee. "I speak for myself and the remainder of the review group. I was the deputy assistant director for the Secret Service's Inspection Division, which would be the equivalent of an internal affairs unit in April of 1993. I was selected to head up this investigation. I was not a volunteer, and I did not have any agenda.

"I went to the Treasury Department," Merletti continued, "and met Mr. Noble and Mr. Moulton, who was the project director. I was told to find the truth."

"Well," Rep. John Conyers Jr. (D-MI) asked, "what have you heard that you took exception to, with one of the witnesses?"

"Yesterday," Merletti told committee members, "one of the witnesses said that this report was unfair, biased, and a cover-up."

"And who was that?" Conyers asked.

"That was Mr. Hartnett [ATF's former deputy director of enforcement]."

"And what is your position," Conyers asked, "that you can vouch from your point of view and experience with this that it was accurate, in fact?"

"It's *absolutely* accurate, sir."

Soon after, Merletti was again challenged about the report's veracity by ATF agents seated at the same table with him and by Rep. Peter Blute (R-MA).

"I'd like to ask Mr. Merletti," Blute began, "to respond, first of all to Mr. Hartnett's strong statement last night, that he felt that this report was flawed, and indeed covered up some of the more damaging statements made by higher-ups. And secondly, I wonder if you'd respond to some of the concerns that [ATF agent] Mr. Sarabyn made in this conversation, which was an extemporaneous conversation between himself and another agent."

Merletti stuck to the report's findings. "Let me say again, I stand by the solid integrity of this report.

"As for Mr. Sarabyn," Merletti countered, "he's referring to the loss of the element of surprise. And upon his arrival at the staging area, he announced, repeatedly, 'We have to hurry up. Koresh knows we're coming.' When I interviewed Chuck Sarabyn, we had already interviewed approximately a hundred people. I had reports from sixty-one individuals, one of them being Mr. Buford [another agent at the table with Merletti], who heard Mr. Sarabyn say, 'Hurry up. Koresh knows we're coming.'

"I asked Mr. Sarabyn, 'Did you say this?' And he said, 'No. I was quoting Mr. Rodriguez.' Once I showed him that we had sixty-one statements, he said, 'Well, I was trying to say what Robert told me.' Later in the interview, he admitted that he knew that Koresh knew the ATF was coming."

The questioning grew more combative with John Mica (R-FL).

"Mr. Merletti," Mica began, "you helped produce this document here [holds up a copy of the report] . . . known as the Treasury report?"

"Yes, sir."

"And on page seven of it," Mica asked, "doesn't it say that the investigation also found disturbing evidence of flawed decision-making, inadequate intelligence gathering, miscommunication, supervisory failures, and deliberately misleading post-raid statements about the raid and the raid plan by certain ATF supervisors? That was your conclusion?"

"Yes, sir."

"And then we had . . . Mr. Daniel Hartnett. He testified . . . that [the] report was filled with distortions, omissions, and, in some cases, things that were simply untrue. 'I believe it was done for political purposes. The politics of the situation became more important than the people involved . . .' [Hartnett said]."

"Sir," Merletti calmly said, "I helped write this report. We did in excess of five hundred interviews. . . . If you recall, right after the raid, the big point was: Was the element of surprise lost or was it not? The line agents stood up and told us the truth. I have *sixty-one* witnesses that said they heard that," Merletti told Mica. "Do you expect me to *ignore* that? That is much more probable cause than I would expect on anything."

On the CBS News program *60 Minutes*, Ron Noble, assistant secretary of the Treasury for Enforcement, reinforced the report's conclusions.

"What was absolutely clear in Washington at Treasury and in Washington at ATF," Noble said, "was that no raid should proceed once the element of surprise was lost. Then the raid planners would have said: 'OK, we can't go forward with the raid.' That's what should have happened. That's what the raid planners were trained to do. That's what they were directed to do, and they didn't do it. That is a mistake. It was a mistake that cost the lives of four Treasury agents."

Sitting at the same table with other ATF agents, Robert Rodriguez, a special agent acting undercover inside the Branch, testified that he told Chuck Sarabyn, his former boss, that Koresh said, "They're coming, Robert. The time has come."

Over at the White House, President Clinton and his staff were viewing the hearing on television.

"They're watching this thing," Merletti said, "because they're thinking, 'Hey, we might get blasted here.' And they said, 'Man, this guy didn't take any guff. He really shot back at them.'"

Near the end of his testimony, Karen Thurman (D-SD) asked Merletti for any additional information that had not come out in the hearing.

Merletti began by recognizing the many acts of bravery and heroism of the men and women of ATF that day in Waco. "I wish that I would have been able to tell all their stories, every one of them. I also want to thank the ATF line agents for stepping up the way they did. It was not easy for them to tell the truth when they realized that they were telling some stories that involved their supervisors that may come back to haunt them."

He ended his testimony with a personal story that caught everyone in the room in a moment of silence.

"Sometimes getting the truth is not pleasant," Merletti said evenly. "When I look back at the hours that we worked and all the travel we did and reliving what a lot of the line agents, members of SRT [Special Response Team], what they went through that day, I wondered, was this worth it?"

Merletti paused, suppressing the emotion of the moment.

"One of the young men that was killed . . . Rob Williams, his father is a Secret Service agent that I work with on occasion. About two months after we put the book out, Tim Williams called me and said, 'I want to thank you for telling the truth about what happened to my son the day he died.'

"*That*," Merletti said softly, "made it worth it."

Merletti's two days of testimony before the subcommittee had left a bitter taste in his mouth. "I saw that the truth is not paramount with these people. They want a soap opera. They want drama."

Clinton invited Merletti over to the White House, along with the secretary of the Treasury, Robert Rubin. "I'm meeting him for the first time, and Clinton says, 'I gotta say, you were up against a heck of fight there. You stood your ground. I'm really proud of you.'"

"Sorry," Merletti told the president, "it's about the truth. I thought they wanted the truth. I find out that it was more of a political thing, and I wasn't going to allow myself to be bullied."

Back at Secret Service headquarters on H Street, Merletti was assigned to Internal Affairs. Meanwhile, Eljay Bowron had been appointed director following John Magaw. At this point, President Clinton had been in office for more than a year.

"A rumor begins," Merletti continued, "that security at the White House isn't the same as it was with Reagan and Bush. The staff does not get along with the Secret Service."

Merletti was called in to see Director Bowron.

"Believe me, every time you get called in to see the director, it's 'Did I do something wrong? Am I being transferred?'"

"Have a seat," Bowron told him. "I am transferring you to the presidential detail."

"I don't want to go there," Merletti told his chief.

"This is not an all-volunteer army," Bowron snapped back. "You're going! We're having some problems there, and you have years of experience, and you're able to get along with presidents. I need you to go there and assess the level of security we have. I'm sending you back, not as the agent in charge, but the deputy agent in charge, the number-two guy. At some point," Bowron said, "you probably will become the agent in charge, but I need you to assess for me what's going on over there."

4

When he returned to the White House, the Secret Service staff kidded the former Reagan/Bush guardian. "Hey, there's a Republican here. We have a Reagan guy."

But over a year and a half, "they came to realize I wasn't about politics. I wasn't about Reagan or Bush. I wasn't about Democrat or Republican. I was about the Secret Service mission to provide protection," Merletti explained.

During his tenure, the Secret Service faced several challenges. On September 12, 1994, Frank Eugene Corder, a despondent thirty-eight-year-old truck driver, stole a Cessna 150 and crashed it onto the South Lawn of the White House. Although Corder was killed in the incident, no other injuries were reported.

Forty-seven days later, twenty-six-year-old Francisco Martin Duran fired twenty-nine rounds from a semiautomatic rifle outside the White House fence before being tackled to the ground by three citizen bystanders as two uniformed Secret Service agents arrested the gunman. Duran was sentenced to forty years.

On December 20, 1994, Marcelino Corniel, a knife-wielding homeless man with a record of violence, was shot and killed in front of the White House. A few months later, Leland William Modjeski was shot and wounded after he scaled the White House fence, brandishing a handgun and threatening to kill the president and Secret Service agents.

However, in November 1996, a more calculated attack was directed at Clinton during the president's visit to the Asia-Pacific Economic Cooperation summit meeting in the Philippines.

As he was leaving a hotel with the president, Merletti, now the special agent in charge of the Presidential Protective Division (PPD), received a message over his radio from intelligence agents who had picked up the words "bridge . . . wedding." Intelligence assessed that an attack against the president was forthcoming and involved the bridge that the presidential motorcade was going to cross on its return to central Manila.

Clinton was already running late for a scheduled meeting in downtown Manila when Merletti gave him the news. "Sir, intelligence has reason to believe that the bridge may not be safe. We'll have to take an alternate route around the island."

A short time later, SRT members discovered that the bridge had been mined. Intelligence later confirmed that Osama bin Laden was behind the attack.

Later that evening, Merletti was summoned to Director Bowron's hotel room.

"Have a seat," Bowron told him. "I'm leaving the Secret Service. I don't know how soon. But I've been looking at all our senior officers. I believe that you have what I'm looking for, and I'm going to recommend you to be the next director. I don't make the final call," Bowron added, "but I will have a lot of input."

"I don't want it," Merletti said.

"What do you mean?"

"Director, I'm over twenty years in the Secret Service. I'm hoping to stay here a little while longer, then put my résumé together. It's time for me to find another career. I don't want to get out of the operational mode. It's what I love."

"Listen," Bowron said, "you have to stop thinking about yourself. You have to start thinking about the United States Secret Service. You have to do this! Look, I'm going to groom you for it. I'm going to move you off the president's detail. I'm going to make you assistant director. You're going to have plenty of time to move into this. I'll still be here to show you the ropes. I'll involve you in everything, and it will be a smooth transition. This will take a couple of years."

"Please," Merletti told his boss, "I'm sure you can find someone else for this—someone qualified who wants the job."

"It was not a contentious meeting," Merletti said. "I was very respectful to him. As he was closing the door, I can still see his face: 'You'll do the right thing.'"

"Six months go by, and I get transferred and I become assistant director," he recalled. "And after a while, I thought [the position as director] just went away. And honestly, I wasn't looking for it.

"One of the things I came to learn from Bowron was 'that was one of the reasons why I wanted you to become the director. There's so much power as director that if you covet that position, it's not good.' He was looking for someone capable that wasn't attracted to it. Someone who would go in and do it.

"Time keeps going by. I'm putting my résumé together. Then Bowron announces his retirement, and I'm selected as one of sixteen to be interviewed."

On June 6, 1997, Lewis C. Merletti was sworn in as the nineteenth director of the United States Secret Service.

Little did the newly appointed director know that in seven months, no amount of training or experience would prepare him for the battle that was yet to come.

5

On January 16, 1998, Monica Lewinsky was rushing to meet Linda Tripp at the Pentagon City shopping mall across the Potomac in Arlington, Virginia. The two friends and former Pentagon coworkers were scheduled to have lunch in the food court at about 1:00 p.m. when two FBI agents approached Lewinsky. After showing their credentials, Tripp faded into the background.

According to a special counsel report examining allegations of professional misconduct by the Office of Independent Counsel—believed to be sealed by the court for almost fourteen years—one of the agents told Lewinsky that "she was in trouble and that she was the subject of a federal criminal investigation."

"Go fuck yourself," Lewinsky responded.

"There are OIC lawyers upstairs," the agent said, "who would tell you about the investigation."

Lewinsky told the agent that he could speak to her attorney.

The agent cautioned that the offer to discuss her legal status was not being given to her attorney but to Lewinsky alone.

The meeting was a setup by Tripp, arranged by Ken Starr and OIC. Based on recorded conversations made by Tripp between herself and Lewinsky, Starr's attorneys wanted to confront Lewinsky about her culpability in criminal activity related to an affidavit she filed in the Paula Jones civil lawsuit against President Clinton. The agents advised Lewinsky that she was not under arrest but that they would like her to accompany them to a room in the hotel to discuss the matter with Starr's attorneys.

After reading author and law professor Ken Gormley's exhaustive work on the Whitewater investigation, *The Death of American Virtue*, I became interested in an interview Gormley conducted with Jo Ann Harris, the former assistant attorney general who led the Criminal Division of the Department of Justice. Retired and teaching law in New York, Harris had been selected by independent counsel Robert Ray, who took over for Starr and was endorsed by Attorney General Reno, to investigate allegations of professional misconduct regarding OIC's covert interview of Lewinsky at the Ritz-Carlton Hotel.

What caught my attention was that despite thousands of pages of documents released to the public concerning the Whitewater and Lewinsky investigations, Harris's investigative report was apparently sealed.

Why?

The crucial aspect of her investigation centered on whether Lewinsky had been appropriately treated by OIC prosecutors when she repeatedly asked to speak to her attorney.

With the report sealed, Harris was prohibited from revealing details. However, in one statement, she told Gormley, "The minute she says, 'Can I call my lawyer?' you stop. And when she says it for the sixth or seventh time, you *really* stop."

And they didn't.

In October 2011, I reached Harris by email through the Elisabeth Haub School of Law at Pace University in New York. She had been traveling between Utah and New York, and although we exchanged emails, it took a full year before I was able to speak with her by phone.

Jo Ann Harris joined the Department of Justice in 1974 as an assistant US attorney prosecuting white-collar crimes in the Southern District of New York. In 1993, Clinton tapped her to become the first woman assistant attorney general of the Criminal Division at DOJ, where she launched the department's Computer Crime and Intellectual Property section and oversaw the initial stages of the investigation into the bombing of the Alfred P. Murrah Federal Building in Oklahoma City in 1995. That same year, Harris received the Division's Henry E. Peterson Memorial Award for exemplary leadership.

During her tenure at the department, it was Harris who encouraged Robert Fiske to take the assignment as the regulatory independent counsel. The two had worked together for four years during their time together at the US Attorney's office in New York.

Harris described Fiske as having a "reputation for fairness, for toughness, for integrity."

Although Harris's report had nothing directly to do with the Secret Service matter, it had everything to do with how Starr's office operated and the key prosecutors involved in decision-making. With her background from DOJ, along with the many OIC attorneys she interviewed, Harris and her report became an invaluable resource for how and why Starr's prosecutors acted the way they did.

At the end of our first conversation, Harris was not only instrumental in helping me begin the process of searching for her report, but candidly shared her opinions about the personalities, as well as the legal and ethical policies, involved.

After a nineteen-month search, I obtained a copy of the hundred-page *Report of the Special Counsel Concerning Allegations of Professional Misconduct by the Office of Independent Counsel in Connection with the Encounter with Monica Lewinsky on January 16, 1998*, by Harris and her co-counsel, Mary Harkenrider.

The December 6, 2000 report by special counsels is really an ethics report. In our interview, Harris made clear to me that although the actions taken by OIC prosecutors may not have been found to constitute professional misconduct—according to the standards and definitions of the Office of Professional Responsibility (OPR)—OIC prosecutors' lack of judgment at critical times compromised their decision-making.

In the fall of 1999, Robert Ray formally took over as head of OIC after Ken Starr returned to private practice. An uncompromising federal prosecutor, Ray would deliver the final decision on both Whitewater and Lewinsky.

During Starr's six-year investigation of Clinton, about ten or twelve complaints were referred to OPR at the department, Harris explained in our interview. Attorney General Reno closed all but the Lewinsky matter. "I think that Ray asked for Lewinsky to be referred back to him to deal with," Harris explained, "and the department said, 'Well, that's all very well and fine, but we would like an independent person doing the investigation.'"

"How could Ray carry out an objective investigation of his own office?" I asked Harris.

"You've actually hit on a very big recommendation of mine, which is that the Office of Independent Counsel be required to have their own OPRs. In other words, their own means of independently investigating each other, because if you believe in the independent counsel concept, the department should not be investigating themselves because that's a conflict of interest."

Early in our conversations, Harris confided that prior to her time at the department, she had "deregistered"—had her name removed from the voting rolls of both parties—to avoid the appearance of bias in her decision-making.

On February 16, 2000, Ray and Reno enlisted Harris to investigate allegations of professional misconduct. Harris's deal with Ray was simple. "I will be your OPR on this subject. We will follow DOJ guidelines on the investigation, just as you are required to follow the guidelines on everything." Harris was told not to disclose that she was working on the Lewinsky matter. "In fact, it was never public record that I was appointed. My friends didn't even know," Harris added.

Before beginning her work, Harris told me that she and Ray had an understanding of her role and the way they would deal with any disagreement. As Ray explained, they would "put both reports out there [Harris's report or summary and Ray's rebuttal] and let the public decide." Based on the evidence, Ray would later decline to honor that understanding.

Between the two of them, Harris and Harkenrider brought some twenty years' experience as prosecutors, including their work at the Department of Justice, to their investigation.

According to Harris, it was Ray's position that the investigation should be able to reach a conclusion regarding OIC's conduct with Lewinsky from documents they submitted to DOJ. However, Harris determined that because of the "strongly adversarial substance and tone," of the documents, "they simply could not be relied upon as a basis for a fair determination of the facts involved."

Due to the "lack of a contemporaneous record, and less than complete and candid after-the-fact submissions," Harris determined that it was necessary to interview virtually all OIC lawyers and agents involved in the brace of Lewinsky "to fully and fairly understand the facts."

Harris maintained that she and Harkenrider were working under the assumption that the investigation and its findings would be made public. However, after submitting her report to Ray, something decidedly changed, surprising the seasoned Justice official and leading me back to the archives as well as the US Court of Appeals. Further research revealed a puzzling and convoluted subplot as to what happened to her report and why.

At the time of her appointment, Harris remembered a few simple instructions given by Reno's office: "Be independent and get it over with."

In the opening to their report, Harris and Harkenrider explain that they were assigned to investigate "allegations that OIC attorneys violated the department's regulation and other policies and rules bearing upon contact by federal prosecutors with persons represented by lawyers."

At the time, Washington attorney Frank Carter was representing Lewinsky in the civil matter regarding Paula Jones, the former Arkansas state employee who sued President Clinton for sexual harassment. The distinction between the civil affidavit that Lewinsky made in the Jones case and the alleged criminal activity posited by OIC and FBI agents who first approached her would become a predominant point later in the inquiry.

At the end of their ten-month investigation, the investigators found that "no lawyer involved in the confrontation with Monica Lewinsky committed professional misconduct." Nonetheless, they concluded that one of Starr's prosecutors, Michael Emmick, "exercised poor judgment and made mistakes in his analysis, planning, and execution of the approach to Lewinsky." They also indicated that OIC attorneys could have better handled the confrontation.

"The entire office knew that Frank Carter represented Lewinsky in the Paula Jones case," Harris said in our conversation. The fact that she had legal counsel "should have set off alarms . . . as OIC prepared to confront and try to 'flip' her. The president of the United States was the eventual target. Intense public scrutiny was inevitable; any misstep would exacerbate the criticism already directed at the office."

In fact, Emmick, a senior prosecutor in the Public Corruption section for the US attorney's office in Los Angeles, who led the brace of Lewinsky, lectured on the issues involved and "specifically knew that a department regulation and related DOJ policies were guiding these types of contacts. He knew as well that those provisions were complicated, not self-evident, highly controversial, and vulnerable to attack from many quarters. The confrontation of Monica Lewinsky demanded a high standard of care and sensitivity."

The special counsels found that Emmick, together with others at OIC, developed a game plan for discouraging Lewinsky "from calling Carter cloaked as a generality: 'If you call anyone, it may hurt your chances to help yourself,'" ultimately resulting in Emmick "offering a Hobson's choice to Lewinsky, and then pushing her for an immediate answer . . . that choice was: 'full immunity, or call the lawyer you desire,' but not both."

At times, the first forty-six pages of the report read like a dark crime novel.

"The doldrums at the Office of Independent Counsel were blown away on Monday evening, January 12, 1998, when Deputy Independent Counsel Jackie Bennett . . . in the Washington office, received a telephone 'tip' from one Linda Tripp. Tripp said that at the urging of the president and his friend Vernon Jordan, a former White House intern was preparing to file a false affidavit in the *Jones v. Clinton* case denying her sexual relationship with the president. Tripp reported that the intern was trying to persuade Tripp to file a false affidavit as well. She later identified the intern as Monica Lewinsky."

Bennett was Starr's right-hand man in the Washington office. Viewed as an "attack dog" by many, the hard-charging attorney "won the Attorney General's John Marshall Award as the top Federal prosecutor of 1994 for convicting Albert Bustamante, a former Representative from Texas, of racketeering and bribery," *The New York Times* reported. Bennett had also worked as a senior trial attorney for DOJ's Public Integrity section, a fact that would become particularly relevant when investigators discussed his interactions with section deputy Josh Hochberg.

"With Lewinsky, OIC had a potentially explosive witness who seemed to be in the middle of committing several federal crimes. She could break open a real case against the president. But the timing of the investigation was being driven, in part, by outside forces and ultimately by a member of the press corps . . . Michael Isikoff of *Newsweek* magazine knew possibly more than OIC lawyers did about the story and, later in the week, began breathing down their necks, threatening to contact the subjects before any law enforcement strategy could be implemented."

Notwithstanding the noir aspects, the report is a critical examination of the abandonment of ethics at decisive times and the rush to get Clinton, no matter the cost.

From the end of December 1997 to early January 1998, Ken Starr's investigation into Clinton's alleged misconduct in the Whitewater Development Corporation was in the process of winding down its work.

"In the words of one of Starr's deputies, 'the issues were long of tooth.'" Many of the more experienced in the office, including Starr, believed that Clinton's delaying tactics had made it impossible for them to make workable cases. "They thought that Clinton was guilty of something and would lie about anything."

It was during this wind-down that Linda Tripp called the Washington office and supplied OIC with the viable lead they'd been looking for. Tripp had worked at the White House before being transferred to a position at the Pentagon, where she became friendly with Lewinsky, a former intern at the White House.

Ken Starr's résumé was impressive including US Solicitor General, and judge of the District of Columbia Court of Appeals. "Highly respected as an appellate lawyer and jurist," the report describes, "Starr had no prosecuting experience when he became independent counsel. Starr's background and experience led to a management style and hiring strategy important to an understanding of the decisions made, how they were made, and who made them in this case.

"Starr emphasizes that he tried to foster a collegial, nonhierarchical structure in the office, calling for the entire legal staff to meet on all important issues, and providing everyone the opportunity to express an opinion. The goal was to develop a decision by consensus."

As Harris explained, Starr's process was not what an experienced prosecutor should do.

"I really believe that many of the people appointed [independent counsels] are ill-suited for the job. They don't have a good sense of what a prosecutor does. They have their own self-righteous sense of 'ethics.' But they don't understand this brown and gray world, and they *don't* understand when they have to say, 'Whoa!' We're dealing in an area where the only thing that controls conduct and enormous power are ethical rules and they're not simple to apply and then rely too much on their staff."

At one point during her interview with the independent counsel, Harris told Starr, "Your staff did not serve you well."

Privately, Harris was more explicit. "I met him when he was solicitor general; very smart, very academic . . . He's a very nice guy, very gentlemanly, very courtly. My sense is—and I've said this countless times—he was way over his head, and he's not the only judge who's been an independent counsel who doesn't have the foggiest notion of how to exercise prosecutorial power, not the foggiest notion. And I think, consequently, his staff ran him.

"The captain of the ship," Harris stressed in our interview, "does not consult with the crew on how to run the ship."

"Starr sought and hired very strong prosecutors from Main Justice and the various United States Attorneys' offices around the country," the report states. "Every OIC lawyer should have known that it was his or her responsibility to follow DOJ policies and to bring issues calling for a review of DOJ policies to the group 'process' established by Starr."

Harris's report then describes what could be termed an administrative blunder: "Starr hired prominent Washington lawyer and law professor Samuel Dash to serve as an ethics consultant and encouraged lawyers to seek his advice on ethics matters."

Dash came to the office of independent counsel with an impeccable pedigree. Nicknamed LSD (Legendary Sam Dash) by many in the office, Dash had been the chief counsel for the Senate Watergate Committee investigating the 1972 break-in of the Democratic National Committee headquarters at the Watergate office complex in Washington, DC. More importantly, he was considered the father of the Independent Counsel Statute, the law that would prevent a sitting president from doing what Richard Nixon had done during Watergate: order the firing of special prosecutor Archibald Cox when Cox, supported by a ruling from John Sirica, US District judge, compelled the president to hand over the secret White House tapes that would eventually lead to Nixon's downfall.

However, Dash says that he was hardly ever consulted by Starr's prosecutors before any action was taken and was not consulted on the Lewinsky matter prior to the brace.

If OIC was going to try to flip Lewinsky, time was running out. They needed to act quickly before Clinton testified in *Jones v. Clinton* on January 17, 1998. Starr and his attorneys "had the unexpected opportunity to conduct an undercover investigation" and potentially catch Clinton in both obstruction of justice regarding Lewinsky and perjury at the *Jones* deposition. However, the question of jurisdiction hung over OIC.

"According to Starr, this issue not only raised esoteric constitutional issues, but as a practical matter, if OIC later was found to have exceeded its jurisdiction, it would have meant disaster for the case," the report states.

Starr's staff had varying opinions. To his credit, "Emmick is quoted by virtually everyone as urging that OIC should 'run, don't walk' to DOJ. Emmick's good judgment on this matter prevailed."

Harris and Harkenrider also investigated the scope of Lewinsky attorney Frank Carter.

"The 1998 Martindale-Hubbell biography of Francis Carter describes an experienced criminal and civil practitioner . . . who had served as a law clerk to the chief judge of the DC Superior Court and, from 1979 to 1985, was the director of the Public Defender Service of the District of Columbia."

Lewinsky "denied having a sexual relationship with the president and urged Carter to get her out of the deposition."

Carter repeatedly cautioned Lewinsky about lying in an affidavit, explaining that "in DC, more people are convicted of covering up" than the original offense. He also warned her about talking to anyone else. "You don't know who is friend, or foe; you can always come to me."

And here is yet another point where OIC's legal strategy veered into questionable ethical territory. Carter believed OIC's confrontation of Lewinsky *did* fall within the scope of his representation. "'They approached her about a clear component of my representation,'" he told special counsels. "Their investigation was totally entwined with my representation."

However, Ken Starr chose to believe a different narrative.

In one of many detailed footnotes, Harris and Harkenrider state, "The way in which Lewinsky ended up with Carter caused some OIC staff to have suspicions that Carter was complicit in the scheme [to lie about Lewinsky's relationship with the president] . . . in Starr's words, it was their '*instinct* based upon experience with the Clinton people.' . . . But there was little evidentiary basis for concluding that Carter was involved in any scheme to commit perjury," and Frank Carter's character was "unimpeachable," Harris told me.

Nonetheless, Starr and many of his prosecutors were so wedded to their assumptions about "the Clinton people" that they ignored statements Lewinsky made to Tripp during their recorded conversations.

Dismissing Carter's recurrent warnings about lying, Lewinsky told Tripp, several times, that she had lied to her attorney, stating that "you cannot tell your own lawyer the truth if you want him to represent you." In another phone call, "Tripp stated that Lewinsky again told Tripp that the thing to do before lying under oath is to lie to your attorney."

Starr's staff had differing opinions as to Carter's involvement. "The [FBI] agents thought he was involved in the crime, as did Starr. On the other hand, Robert Bittman, a deputy independent counsel assigned to Little Rock at the time, consulting by telephone, acknowledged that they had information from Tripp that Lewinsky was misleading Carter and that there was no real evidence on him. Bennett says they had 'no reason to believe whether Carter was straight or crooked,' adding 'We had never heard of Frank Carter.'"

Nonetheless, Starr went all in, believing Carter was involved in the deception.

A simple background check on Carter would have revealed much about the man and his reputation. However, there was no indication to suggest that anyone at OIC ever attempted to find out who Carter was before approaching Lewinsky.

On Thursday, January 15, 1998, *Newsweek* reporter Michael Isikoff—who, according to Starr, was "breathing fire and brimstone" and "a pain in the neck"—was still pressing to run the Lewinsky story, a bombshell that remained unknown to the public. Two days later, the story would break in the Drudge Report, an online gossip site at the time.

"[Isikoff told OIC] that the White House was aware of inquiries about Lewinsky and warned that he was going to start making calls that day. In the end, after Bennett described the harm to the investigation of any overt inquiries, Isikoff agreed to hold off until 4:00 p.m. on Friday."

Within twenty-four hours, Bennett told investigators, "They lost the initiative in the timing of the approach to Lewinsky, and the pressure caused 'triage in analysis.'"

6

On Thursday morning, "OIC staff began brainstorming how to approach Lewinsky . . . the stronger personalities dominated the discussion," the report states. "Others tell us there was a clash as to who was in charge and that Emmick and [Bruce] Udolf [a senior federal corruption prosecutor from the Miami US Attorney's office] 'glommed' on to the case. [An FBI agent], noting that no one seemed to be in charge of the case, says that OIC staff still seemed to be working on the jurisdictional issues for a meeting with [Deputy Attorney General] Holder later that day."

At that meeting, OIC made its case before Holder, believing they had additional jurisdiction and would win the approval of the Department of Justice for that position. Soon after, Lee J. Radek, the chief of the department's Public Integrity section, was called in. "Known for his street savvy, lawyerly acumen, and good judgment," *Time* magazine wrote, Radek worked at the newly created section of the criminal Division two years after the Watergate scandal.

Radek charged one of his deputies, Josh Hochberg, to go to OIC offices to help the Justice Department determine the jurisdictional issue. It was at a meeting between Hochberg and OIC where Starr's lawyers were presented with alternatives but chose not to take them.

"Hochberg suggested that if OIC had concerns about Carter's reliability or complicity, they should serve Lewinsky with a grand jury subpoena, which would bring the question of Carter's possible conflict before a court for determination. Such a strategy would have placed Carter in a position that bound him not to reveal what was happening or face allegations of obstruction of the grand jury."

Hochberg also raised DOJ's regulation regarding contacting a person who has a lawyer and told OIC prosecutors "that if he were they, he would not go forward without first seeking the guidance and protection provided by DOJ through the *Margolis* procedure, a process established by the department to help federal prosecutors evaluate issues involving the regulation proscribing [forbidding] contacts with represented people, on a case-by-case basis. By using the process, prosecutors not only received advice from department experts, but obtained authority to proceed, thus providing protection from later charges of abuse."

However, Harris notes that although he "had a great deal of respect [for Hochberg], Starr did not recall that Hochberg said anything about DOJ process or procedure regarding the contacts regulation and did not recall any statement regarding a *Margolis* procedure."

In another special counsel interview, Starr's chief deputy, Jackie Bennett, had been "a trial lawyer in the Public Integrity section, [and] was aware of the contacts issue . . . 'I was pretty confident,' [Bennett said], 'that I could spot the issue and go for help.' When we asked about the

Margolis procedure for doing just that, he said that it sounded familiar. Later in the interview, Harris directly asked if Bennett remembered Hochberg raising the *Margolis* process. Bennett did not remember."

Although the procedure may have been familiar to Bennett, he and others took no steps to utilize a method that would have eliminated any questions that would have compromised OIC's decision-making.

The report notes:

Starr . . . returned to the subject of jurisdiction and told Hochberg that he believed OIC had "ancillary" jurisdiction but that he wanted DOJ concurrence. Ultimately, Starr gave Hochberg a letter to take back to DOJ. In it, [Starr] asserted once again that OIC had "related" jurisdiction but sought the department's opinion and a referral to OIC if the department concluded to the contrary.

With this letter, Starr now believed that OIC had the legal authority to confront Lewinsky.

That evening, as Bennett walked by Michael Emmick's office, he asked the man who would ultimately question Lewinsky, "I know you are the contacts guy. Are there any contacts problems here?"

Emmick sat back and "after about five [to] ten seconds said, 'One, she's not represented here; and two, it's pre-indictment. No problem. [Carter is] her lawyer in a civil proceeding; his representation is to the affidavit in the civil case; whatever arrangement they have, it is in the civil proceeding.'"

Thus, Emmick regarded Carter "just like any other person, not Lewinsky's lawyer." This position, Harris and Harkenrider concluded, "colored all that occurred thereafter."

Emmick's judgment not only conflicted with Carter's, that "OIC's 'investigation was totally entwined with my representation,'" but also with the opinion of some of OIC's prosecutors, notably Lewinsky chief investigator Robert Bittman.

Many of Starr's prosecutors clung to their belief that "Clinton was guilty of something and would lie about anything."

As Harris explained to me, all of Starr's attorneys had a duty to proceed ethically regarding Lewinsky and relied on Emmick's guidance on the issue. Bennett's mindset was that OIC had examined the issue and concluded that it was unnecessary to get DOJ's approval, "we are our own office," a reference to the premise of the Independent Counsel Act.

OIC arranged to have Tripp meet with Lewinsky at the Pentagon City shopping mall in Virginia the following day. Tripp would guide Lewinsky to two FBI special agents, Patrick Fallon and Steve Irons, who would try to convince her to go with them to a room in the Ritz-Carlton, where she would be confronted with the evidence of her crimes, and they would attempt to flip her.

"There was no script for the agents' confrontation," investigators point out, "but the agents who were 'gaming' by themselves on Thursday night concluded that if Lewinsky asked for her lawyer, he would be contacted and the confrontation would be lawyer-to-lawyer thereafter."

Harris emphasized that "the agents who conducted the brace on Lewinsky were not happy with the process, or with the lawyers they were dealing with. OIC had no clear playbook in terms of what the agents ought to say, in terms of how they wanted to deal with the whole thing. The agents were just not part of the team."

On the evening before the confrontation, Bennett, Emmick, and Udolf met to discuss the plan. It included offering Lewinsky a "cooperation-made-known" deal, in which the quality of her cooperation would be taken into account and made known to the sentencing judge. If Lewinsky asked about contacting a lawyer, "they would say that if she were to contact anyone, there was a risk she would be exposed and lose her chance to cooperate."

A key point Harris made clear to me is that "no one seems to have taken any steps at this time to try to determine whether this was a proper means of discouraging her from contacting Carter, whether other means might be available, or whether encouraging her to forego contacting Carter was appropriate at all."

Later that evening, Emmick began to script out his presentation and distributed it to other attorneys in the office.

After a high-level meeting at DOJ, it was decided that OIC needed an expansion to proceed.

"There are two ways that the independent counsel can expand the jurisdiction that the court gives them," Harris explained: "one, they could've declared it themselves as related, or they could get the department's referral, and it was very important for Starr to get the department to agree. "It was *terribly* important," she stressed. "If they'd gone ahead without that confidence, there might have been an entirely different kind of litigation going on."

In fact, when expansion into the Lewinsky matter was first raised in the office, it was *Starr* who insisted that they needed a referral from DOJ. Starr believed, and made clear to his attorneys, that "it was important to be covered with 'belt and suspenders' for sensitive matters such as this."

On the morning of the Lewinsky encounter, Hochberg, along with his boss from DOJ, Lee Radek, arrived at OIC. Awaiting Starr's arrival, DOJ attorneys had a conversation with three OIC attorneys and Michael Emmick, designated as the "speaker" who would confront Lewinsky in the hotel room. Hochberg and Radek were told that the office had listened to more of Tripp's conversations with Lewinsky and concluded that "it contained even stronger and more explicit evidence of witness tampering."

However, as special counsels note, "unnoticed, ignored, or simply regarded as not relevant in this taped conversation is Tripp's comment to Lewinsky that 'you didn't even tell your own attorney the truth. . . ,' indicating again that Carter was not in on the scheme."

After Starr arrived, he and Radek called David B. Sentelle, the presiding judge of the Special Division. They explained that the matter involved "an emergency investigative situation and asked for a verbal order expanding OIC's jurisdiction" into the Lewinsky matter. Sentelle said he would consult with his two colleagues and get back to Radek.

A half hour later, Sentelle authorized the expansion Starr was seeking, and OIC prepared to move forward with the brace of Lewinsky.

Linda Tripp had arranged to meet Lewinsky at 12:30 p.m. at Pentagon City. OIC reserved two rooms at the Ritz-Carlton. FBI agents had phone and body equipment ready. The plan would entail Tripp to be wired and if "Monica stops interview midstream . . . we'll have Linda come in screaming and they leave together, [Tripp] taping.'"

Harris told me that although this suggestion again indicated that the agents had concerns about what to do if Lewinsky asked for her lawyer, there was no further discussion of other potential courses of action.

FBI Special Agent Steve Irons told investigators that Starr's office was haphazard and likened the operations at OIC to "kids playing a game of T-Ball." Rather than sticking to their assignments, everyone was drawn to the action of the moment.

At this point, Hochberg met with OIC prosecutors a third time. According to notes taken, the meeting's focus was on Hochberg's question as to what OIC would do if Lewinsky asked for an attorney, as follows:

[FBI agent]: "Going to advise her of her rights, keep a log. Won't arrest. Will tell her she's free to leave anytime."

Josh [Hochberg]: "What if she wants an attorney?"

[FBI agent]: "Okay. Don't say a word. Just listen to me for five minutes."

(Josh looks skeptical)

[FBI agent]: "We'll explain the evidence. Do you still want an attorney?"

Mike [Emmick]: "We can tell her that if she has an attorney, she gets lesser rewards—concern about our ability to work undercover."

Josh: "This is a criminal investigation—as far as we know, you're not represented in this. It would be to your benefit to hear us out."

Ken [Starr]: "Are you comfortable with that?"

Josh: "I don't love it. But I'm satisfied."

However, the notes "do not record any reaction to Michael Emmick's suggestion that if Lewinsky asked about calling her lawyer, they would say that it would decrease the value to her of cooperation, and it became the centerpiece of OIC's strategy to keep Lewinsky from calling Carter," and no log of the conversation with Lewinsky was ever kept by agents.

Why didn't Hochberg more vigorously question OIC's strategy?

Hochberg told Harris and Harkenrider that he was uncomfortable in his meetings with OIC but repeated several times to investigators "this was OIC's investigation and in light of the independence required by the law, he did not feel he should, or could, stop them from any course of action."

At this point, Emmick and Udolf, headed over to the Ritz-Carlton before 1:00 p.m. Riding separately from the agents, Emmick cautioned his colleague "to be especially careful not to cross the ethical line."

When asked to clarify by investigators, Emmick said that they should not, in any way, criticize Lewinsky attorney, Frank Carter.

"It would appear," the report states, "that there had never been a meeting of the minds between the agents and the lawyers as to roles and strategy, nor was there a final meeting at the hotel. According to Udolf, the plan was 'a work in progress . . . we had to wing it.'"

If Lewinsky attempted to lie to prosecutors, Irons "had the tape [of her conversation with Tripp] cued-up and was prepared to play it for Lewinsky." However, Irons noted that, "as the day played out, she was apparently never confronted with the evidence against her. It became clear to him that OIC attorneys simply didn't know the facts."

Fallon and Irons arrived at the food court at around 1:00 p.m. As Irons approached Lewinsky with his badge out, Tripp faded into the background. Irons advised Lewinsky that she was in trouble, and the subject of a criminal investigation. "This is not about Paula Jones," Irons said."

"Go fuck yourself," Lewinsky said.

Irons explained that she was not under arrest but that "agents and attorneys wished to discuss her culpability in criminal activity related to the Paula Jones civil lawsuit."

"I'm not talking with you without my lawyer," Lewinsky said.

Irons explained, that if Lewinsky wanted her lawyer, "we won't give him as much information, and you won't be able to help yourself as much." After the agents reiterated that she was not under arrest and "free to leave," she followed them upstairs shortly after 1:00 p.m.

"The written record of what occurred between 1:05 p.m., when Lewinsky arrived in room 1012, and when she left with her mother almost twelve hours later is sketchy at best," investigators write.

"When asked about this sparse record, Emmick stated that he saw no need for notes during his 'pitch,' [and] says he assumed the FBI would take any notes necessary during the day. [He] says that he suggested to Starr the next day that they all write memos about the events of January 16."

However, neither Emmick nor anyone else at OIC completed such a memo.

As soon as Irons introduced Lewinsky to Emmick, she once again insisted that she talk to her attorney, Frank Carter.

"Why don't you hear us out," Emmick replied, "and then decide whether you want to call him."

Harris repeated to me what she stressed to author Ken Gormley. "The minute she says, 'Can I call my lawyer?' you stop."

Emmick did not recall any of this, besides, he told investigators, "it was pre-indictment anyway. Even if she had said that [Carter] represents me in the criminal case, it would not have made a difference in his assessment."

Emmick's conclusion "that pre-indictment contact was always allowed, was simply wrong," investigators point out.

Emmick began his pitch to Lewinsky in a sociable manner. Fallon described it as the "wine and cheese" approach.

After several minutes, Emmick pivoted, "stating that it was an OIC investigation and that it involved the Paula Jones case. . . . Lewinsky says that Emmick told her . . . the case involved perjury, obstruction of justice, witness tampering, subornation of perjury [persuading someone to make a false oath as part of a judicial proceeding], and conspiracy. He told her that if she cooperated, the government could bring no charges at all or file something with a judge who could reduce her sentence to no jail time or probation, depending on the value of her cooperation. Lewinsky remembers that [he] kept telling her that the matter was time sensitive.

"Between periods of crying and feeling 'completely freaked out' Lewinsky asked a number of questions about 'cooperation made known' and about calling her attorney, Frank Carter."

"The fewer people who know, the better off you are," an agent told her.

Emmick explicitly told Lewinsky that they didn't want her to contact Carter because he may be involved in criminal activity.

However, Harris explained Emmick's real purpose to me. "They were not concerned so much about Carter's complicity in the crime. That's what they told Lewinsky. They were concerned about him telling the Clinton people."

With reporter Michael Isikoff's deadline approaching, Emmick offered Lewinsky full immunity for full cooperation. However, Lewinsky still had questions: "Should I get an attorney regarding the immunity thing? I don't understand why Carter being my attorney in the Paula Jones case doesn't make him my attorney on this. [If] there is a difference in the criminal and civil case, what kind of attorney should I get? I might want Frank Carter for this. Wouldn't Carter be good? Can't he do criminal law? At one point, Lewinsky suggested taking a taxi to her attorney's office."

One of the agents told Lewinsky that Carter was a civil attorney representing her in a civil case, and that she needed an attorney with experience in federal criminal law. However, simple homework would have revealed that Carter practiced both civil and criminal law.

Clearly, both the agents and Starr's attorneys were steering Lewinsky away from contacting her attorney. The report states that both Emmick and an agent clarified to Lewinsky "that the civil and criminal cases were separate, and that Lewinsky could not be represented in the criminal case because she did not know about it and it was a work in progress."

Although OIC lawyers and FBI agents may not have crossed any legal boundaries, they were taking advantage of Lewinsky's lack of legal knowledge to both dissuade her from contacting Carter and persuade her to fully cooperate in an undercover scheme to trap Clinton.

What troubled investigators most was—absent any background research on Carter—Michael Emmick "did nothing to avert the implication regarding Carter's experience."

As Harris explained to me, "It's one thing not to analyze a very complicated department policy about 'contacts with represented persons' and whether or not Carter fit into that, but it's quite another when a person repeatedly talks about different ways of contacting their lawyer . . . I can't think of a prosecutor who would not just *stop* after this.

"Incidentally," Harris added, "that tough little lady never folded . . . clearly bullied . . . she never folded. She never gave them anything. She kept trying to negotiate with them."

The report cites a 1979 federal case (*US v. Weiss*, 599 F. 2d at 741) in which the presiding judge asserted:

> The citizen's choice of, and relation with, his attorney is none of the investigating government's business. It does not become the government's business because it fears the citizen will tell his attorney of his conversation with government counsel . . . Nor can the government justify its intrusion on the ground it suspects the attorney of wrongdoing related to the matter under investigation.

"At approximately 3:00 p.m., Lewinsky wanted to talk to someone else, her attorney, or her mother, before making a decision."

To pacify Lewinsky, prosecutors gave her the number of the Legal Aid Society. However, Lewinsky did not trust any of the attorneys in the room.

Deadlocked, Emmick called in a reinforcement, Jackie Bennett, who told Lewinsky that time was running out.

Bennett was blunt. "You're twenty-four, you're smart, you're old enough, you don't need to call your mommy."

"Well, if you're not going to let me call my attorney, and you're not going to let me call my mom, I'm leaning against cooperating," Lewinsky told the tough prosecutor,

Bennett said something like: "You need to know that we're going to prosecute your mother as well for what the tapes said she did."

Bennett "got pissed," Lewinsky told Harris.

With that, Starr's chief deputy left the room.

Frustrated by their complete lack of progress, the attorneys allowed Lewinsky to go downstairs to call her mother without losing the immunity agreement. When Harris and Harkenrider asked why she didn't call Carter at that point, Lewinsky said that "she was afraid she was being followed, that the downstairs phones were tapped, and that she would lose the opportunity to help herself.

"Lewinsky returned to the room at approximately 4:12 p.m. and finally reached her mother, Marcia Lewis, by phone. Lewis told Emmick that she would travel to Washington by train to meet with them at the hotel."

With her mother en route, Lewinsky asked if the immunity offer would remain valid if she contacted Carter. Emmick explained "that complete immunity required complete cooperation and meant that 'we don't want you talking to anybody.' He told her that she could go back to cooperation made known" if she wanted to call Carter.

The issue of contacting Carter was raised by a juror in Lewinsky's grand jury testimony.

"Did they ever tell you that you could not call Mr. Carter?" the juror asked.

"No," Lewinsky replied. "What they told me was that if I called Mr. Carter, I wouldn't necessarily still be offered an immunity agreement."

"And did you feel threatened by that?"

"Yes," Lewinsky said.

Lewinsky never called Carter.

Lewinsky's mother arrived late that evening, and after speaking with her daughter and the lawyers, she called her former husband, Lewinsky's father, Bernard Lewinsky. A short time later, Bernard

Lewinsky told Starr's attorneys that William Ginsburg now represented his daughter.

The evening ended past midnight, and so did OIC's hopes of obtaining Lewinsky's cooperation. "Months of negotiation would pass before Lewinsky was eventually given the full immunity offered to her by Emmick and Udolf on January 16, 1998."

7

While OIC was quietly attempting to flip Lewinsky, on January 17, 1998, the Drudge Report alerted the world to the news of the alleged affair.

Four days later, Secret Service director Lewis Merletti was driving to work when he heard National Public Radio (NPR) reporters Robert Siegel and Mara Liasson interviewing President Clinton.

"Is there any truth to the allegation of an affair between you and the young woman?" Siegel asked.

Merletti couldn't believe what he was hearing. He was the special agent in charge of the president's detail at the time and had never heard a word from any of his agents about any association between Clinton and Lewinsky.

"When the entire Monica Lewinsky thing hit," Merletti recalled, "I was the director, and things were going well. I was working to maintain the same high standards for the service that the previous directors had.

Then, I'm driving to work and hear the news about an allegation that he had an affair with this intern, and I thought, What?

"Then it starts coming out, a day or two later, that Secret Service agents may be involved. *What?*

"The weekend gets here, and it's become a huge diversion. I'm no longer focusing on how the Secret Service stops terrorists, how we prevent Osama bin Laden from getting an edge on us. A large part of my time *every* day is dealing with this issue.

"It was the first Sunday. In my home, downstairs, I have a small gym. When I go down to work out, the light bulb goes out. I call up to my son to bring down another bulb. As my eyes are adjusting to the light, I see a box sitting there and I wonder, 'What is this?' I reach in and grab a handful of stuff. My son comes down with a light bulb and a flashlight. He flips the flashlight on; I look, and in my hand is a letter addressed to me, and the return address says, 'Monica Lewinsky.'

"The letter is dated October 28, 1996. Now, this was written before I'm the director. It's written when I was the agent in charge at the White House. The whole affair is over. She's no longer at the White House."

Merletti explained that he got the letter while at the White House. Inside were photos of him from *The New York Times Magazine*. During the presidential campaign, the Secret Service had agreed to allow the magazine to shadow both the president's detail and Senator Robert Dole's.

"So, this was a story being written about us. I put it back in the envelope and throw it in my desk and never looked at it again. When I get transferred, I bring a cardboard box to my desk and empty the stuff in the desk. I take the box home and just forget about it.

"Now, over a year later, I reach in that box, and I pull this letter out. So now it has huge significance to me. In reality, this is what saved me."

28 October 1996

Dear Agent Merletti,

While I don't think you would know me by name, Monica Lewinsky, I am quite sure you would know me by sight . . . I used to work at the White House in Legislative Affairs and transferred over to the Pentagon about six months ago. I was always walking back and forth from the East Wing to the West Wing and am loquacious by nature, so I was always engaging whichever agent was outside the Oval in conversation. Since my move over to the Pentagon, I have seen you at some of the functions. You might recall that I used to tease you about being in all of the pictures of the president . . .

Well, I was glancing through this past week's *New York Times Magazine* and read this article on the Secret Service. I was happy to see that you have become famous in your own right! Looking at these pictures, this time it was the president making a cameo in your photograph rather than the other way around!!!

Thank you for doing such a great job of protecting the "Big Guy," and take care!

—Monica Lewinsky.

Merletti showed the letter to Kelleher, who instantly reacted. "My God, we have to turn this over to Ken Starr."

"When I brought the letter in," Merletti described, "it was like, let's take a look at the date; let's take a look at what she says. In the letter, she says that I don't even know her by name. Now, how would I be doing all this stuff [arranging liaisons between Clinton and Lewinsky]?

Why would she even write this letter if she knew me so well? She's not a suspect. She's just John Q. Citizen."

In OIC's third interview with Lewinsky an FBI agent records: "Lewinsky saw a USSS plainclothes agent named Lou Merletti several times but had more of an acquaintance than a friendship with him. Merletti gave Lewinsky his business card. Lewinsky teased Merletti about being in so many photos with the president and sometimes joked with him in the hallways."

"That's not true at all," Merletti said. "I was never in the hallways. Agents were standing post. I didn't stand post."

"*Lewinsky saw Merletti at the Nutcracker in December 1996.*"

"That was true," Merletti said.

"*Merletti was very friendly with Lewinsky and she sent him a letter once. Merletti never saw Lewinsky with the president, to her knowledge.*"

As Merletti recalled, "Ken Starr wasn't happy to hear about this, because now this puts a big hole in my 'hiding him under a blanket' story."

Leaving OIC after his first meeting with Starr, Merletti told Kelleher that he wanted a meeting with Attorney General Reno. He wanted to stop any further actions by the independent counsel before they could get started and felt that Reno would look at his presentation and clearly understand the stakes involved.

However, before that meeting, Merletti scheduled a conference with all living former Secret Service directors.

"When I made my first presentation to Starr, I was in a most unique situation. I was the director of the Secret Service, so I'm leading the organization. The organization must take a stance. But I'm also the former agent in charge of the president's detail during the period that the Lewinsky affair allegedly happened. So, I must make sure that it's in the interest of the Secret Service, not in the interest of Lew Merletti, who was the agent in charge. I did nothing wrong there," Merletti stressed. "I knew none of this stuff about Lewinsky, but I also realized that this could look like Lew Merletti trying to cover his tracks. 'He witnessed all this and never did anything about it.'

"I don't want my decisions made in a vacuum, so, I call in the four former living directors of the Secret Service into my office."

After listening to Merletti detail Starr's plans to subpoena agents to testify about the president's personal life, John R. Simpson, the Service's sixteenth director, was the first to speak.

"Let me explain something to you. You see that chair?" Simpson said forcefully, pointing to the director's chair at the other end of the room. "When I sat in that chair, this Secret Service lived on the principle of *being worthy of Trust and Confidence*,' and I think I speak for all the other directors here, agreed?"

Everyone in the room spoke with one voice: "Absolutely!"

"You can't back down," former director Stuart Knight added.

"You're being challenged," Simpson said. "You know what you have to do!"

As they were leaving the meeting, one of the formers placed his hand on Merletti's shoulder. "You're the first to be tested. Don't let us down."

Former director John Magaw confirmed the meeting.

With the full support from the former directors as well as the former special agents in charge of the president's detail, Merletti and Kelleher walked into a conference room at DOJ expecting to confer with

Janet Reno. Instead, the room was packed with "a minimum of fifteen attorneys. Janet Reno doesn't come in," Merletti described. "They said, 'You have an hour and a half to make your case.'"

As he stood to begin a PowerPoint presentation, Merletti observed that all the attorneys had their arms folded in body language that telegraphed, prove it to me.

"About a third of the way through, all of a sudden, the arms are uncrossed," Merletti demonstrated. "They're listening. This wasn't rocket science. This is what history has shown us.

"By the end of my presentation, the attorneys were saying, 'He's right . . . makes sense . . . Did Starr see this?'"

Kelleher and Merletti returned to Secret Service headquarters. Sometime in the next couple of hours, they got a phone call. "Come back tomorrow," a department official tells Merletti. "You *are* going to see Janet Reno."

The next day, Merletti and Kelleher returned to the same room at the department. Five attorneys from the previous day were there, along with a group of new attorneys. Janet Reno and Eric Holder walked in last.

"OK, Lew," Holder said, signaling Merletti.

"The level of protection provided the president of the United States is unparalleled in terms of intensity and scope. No mayor, no governor, no prime minister, or any other world leader receives the same level of protection or receives the overwhelming number of threats or attempts on their lives."

Descriptive slides on Merletti's laptop matched his presentation as department attorneys listened and watched closely.

"Ten of the last eleven American presidents have been the target of assassination. Nine of those ten were stalked or attacked by at least two deadly would-be assassins. Two of the last eight were shot; one was killed; one was seriously wounded. At one point in our history, we had three presidents killed in thirty-six years.

"Proximity to our protectees," Merletti emphasized, "is the heart and soul of our protective mission. Having trust and confidence allows for that proximity. *Proximity* is the difference between life and death to our protectees. This agency has a long history of protection."

Merletti brought up a drawing illustrating the first in a series of assassination attempts against US presidents.

"President Andrew Jackson, January 30, 1835. No security present; Richard Lawrence, within feet of the president, drew a gun; it misfired. He drew a second gun; it misfired. What were the odds? The president was a very lucky man that day.

"President Abraham Lincoln, April 14, 1865. No security present; John Wilkes Booth shoots Lincoln from less than six inches. Had security been in proximity, the course of history may not have been changed."

Merletti continued through slides describing Presidents Garfield and McKinley before clicking on a video showing the attempt on President Ronald Reagan. Everyone's eyes were fixed on the screen.

"President Ronald Reagan, March 30, 1981. Washington, DC; John Hinckley Jr. fires six shots. Special agent Tim McCarthy does *exactly* what he was trained to do—he uses his body as a shield to prevent Hinckley from killing the president," Merletti described. "Standing next to Reagan, special agent Jerry Parr quickly moves the president into the limo and speeds away. Agent McCarthy was seriously wounded during the attack. Due to their proximity history was not changed by an assassin's bullet."

Another series of slides detailed events in 1963 that DOJ officials were unfamiliar with.

"President John F. Kennedy, November 18, 1963. Four days *before* Dallas," Merletti explained as he clicked to another slide with an enlarged inset showing two agents on the back bumper of Kennedy's limo.

"That's special agent Clint Hill and another agent, on the back bumper of the president's limo. The President ordered the agents off the back of the car. Kennedy said that the agents were creating a barrier between the people and the president.

"November 22, 1963, Dallas, Texas."

The slide showed Clint Hill outlined in a red circle.

"Here's Special Agent Hill on the back bumper in Dallas, the day Kennedy was assassinated. In preparing this presentation, Agent Hill told me that he had sensed that something was wrong. Per the president's order, he steps off the presidential limo and returns to the follow-up car."

Another slide from Dallas showed red circles around the empty grab bars on the rear of Kennedy's limo.

"Moments before the president is shot, you can see the grab bars on the back of his limo. There are no agents there."

Merletti brought up the 8mm film showing the final moments. Taken by eyewitness Abraham Zapruder, the film has become iconic in Kennedy assassination lore.

The director said nothing, letting the silent film play what has now become familiar to us all. To this day, the grainy, saturated Kodachrome images remain heart-stopping. Everyone in the room was silent, motionless, riveted to the screen.

"Had both agents been allowed proximity"—they were all watching the final shot to Kennedy—"the course of history may not have been changed by an assassin.

"Secret Service history has proven that confidentiality affords us the proximity that is critical to the success of our mission.

"*Proximity*," Merletti again emphasized, "is the difference between life and death to our protectees. If our protectees cannot trust us; if they believe that they will be called to testify before a grand jury to reveal confidences, the president will not allow us that critical proximity.

"I speak for an hour and a half to two hours," Merletti said, "and halfway through, people are going, 'He's right!'"

Everyone's attention was drawn to one final video—a *60 Minutes* interview of Clint Hill by journalist Mike Wallace.

Before his presentation, Merletti had met with Hill to discuss a rarely seen photo of him on the back bumper of the president's limo on November 22, 1963—in later images, he's not there. Merletti showed me the photo of the Kennedy motorcade from November 18. The photo shows agents kneeling on the back of the car.

I looked at the photo more closely. "I've never seen this before."

"No one has ever seen this before. We are not trained, *ever*, to kneel down like this.

"Here's what happened. They're in this motorcade in Tampa, and the president leans forward to this guy." Merletti indicated the agent sitting on the passenger side of the limo. "The guy in the right front seat is the supervisor. And the president will know who that guy is. They have a relationship. President Kennedy leans forward to the supervisor and says, 'I don't want the agents on the back of the car anymore. Get them off.'

"He radios back to them, 'The president said, "Get off the car."' Now, first, this is old-generation protection," Merletti explained. "If the president of the United States told me to tell the guys to get off the car, I'd say, 'Sir, it's none of your concern.' But this is old-generation Secret Service."

In Tampa, however, "he radios them to get off the car. Well, the car's going about twenty miles an hour. If you jump off, you're going right down. So, they stay on the car, but they're standing. Two, three minutes go by, and Kennedy leans forward again and says, 'I want them off the car.'

"He radios back, 'Get off the car.'

"They radio back, 'We can't! When you slow down, we'll get off.'

"To keep a lower profile, they kneel down. Now, that's got to be painful if they're kneeling on a hard, steel running board. This is the photo that catches them up close.

"So, now, the advance team is down in Dallas. The agents in Dallas are told, 'The president has ordered us off the car. We're not allowed on that car anymore. We're only allowed to be on the follow-up car.'"

"Four days *before*—" I repeated.

"—the Kennedy assassination," Merletti said.

"Now, the next photo, again, a shocker. This is Clint Hill. Are you familiar with who he is?"

"Yes." The image and name of Clint Hill are forever embedded in the minds of most Americans familiar with that day in Dallas. Merletti handed me another photo I was unfamiliar with that showed Hill crouching down on the back bumper of the presidential limo in Dallas.

"I called Clint in," Merletti said. "'Clint, you know we're being challenged by Ken Starr. I'm trying to put a presentation together to talk about the possibility of us being pushed away. To begin with, could you tell me what you are doing here?' I pointed to the photo. 'How did you end up on the back of the car, four days later?'"

"Lew," Hill recalled, "I hoped that this picture would never come out. I'm on the follow-up car, and I knew I was not allowed on that limousine. All of us knew that. I can't tell you what it was, Lew, a sixth sense, but something was wrong that day. I don't know if people were too close, or the crowds were too big. I didn't think that the president was going to be shot. I just didn't feel comfortable. The next thing I know, I come off the follow-up car and get on the president's limo, and I know I'm not allowed there. So, I get right off and go back to the follow-up car.

"Within minutes," Hill said, "it's overpowering, again . . . something *is* wrong. So, I come off the follow-up car and go back to the limo. I did it three times. The photo you caught is about a minute before the first shot is fired. I go back to the follow-up car and I hear it . . ." Hill made a clapping sound with his hands. "I knew, right in my gut."

Moving his head to the left, Hill described to Merletti, "I had to come all the way around, and I actually saw the barrel coming back in and I could see smoke. I knew he was shot."

"You see, there's still controversy about this," Merletti said. "He believes the first shot missed, totally."

"I came off the follow-up car and I'm digging in," Hill recalled. "In my mind's eye, I'm seeing a guy working a bolt, coming back down for the second shot. I'm digging in with everything I've got, and I hear the second shot. It came from the *exact* same spot. The second shot is when the president goes like this . . ."

Hill mimicked Kennedy's hands to his throat.

"Now, I *know* he's hit. With every muscle fiber I have, I'm digging into the pavement. I'm trying to get to that car. I don't know, is the guy reloading again? Is another one coming? I'm getting closer and closer. I'm almost there and . . . [Hill claps his hands, again] . . . the president's head vaporized in front of me. I knew at that moment he was dead."

Starr's insistence on agent testimony would undercut protection, open the door to the likelihood of another presidential assassination. All that lived in the back of Merletti's mind as he listened to Hill.

"Had me and the other agent been standing there [on the bumper], one of several things would have happened. Either Oswald would have had no shot, or he'd have shot one of us, or maybe he'd have shot, but we'd have stood a chance."

Hill lingered, staring into his past. "We failed our mission. The president died, and it was my fault."

"It wasn't your fault," Merletti told him.

"It was my fault. Every night when I put my head on the pillow those demons come and visit me. I live this assassination every day."

After decades of replaying the scene thousands of times in his head, the former agent continued to bear the intense personal responsibility for the assassination in Dallas.

"Lew," Hill told his director, "don't let Ken Starr do this. We got pushed away by the president. Don't let another agent follow in my footsteps. Promise me that you'll fight this."

"I promise."

"And I will be by your side at every court appearance," Hill added.

Reno closely watched the *60 Minutes* piece.

"Was there anything that the Secret Service or that Clint Hill could have done to keep that from happening?" Wallace asked.

"Clint Hill, yes," the former Kennedy agent softly said.

"What do you mean?"

"If [I'd] reacted about five-tenths of a second faster, or maybe a second faster, I wouldn't be here today."

"You mean, you would've gotten there, and you would've taken the shot," Wallace said.

"The third shot, yes sir."

"And that would've been all right with you?"

"That would've been fine with me."

"But you couldn't. You got there in less than two seconds, Clint. You couldn't have gotten there [any earlier]. You surely don't have any sense of guilt about that?"

"Yes, I certainly do," Hill told Wallace. "I have a great deal of guilt about that. Had I turned in a different direction, I'd have made it. It's my fault."

Wallace tried to reassure him. "Oh, no one has ever suggested that for an instant. What you did was show great bravery and great presence of mind. What was on the citation that was given you: *For your work on November 22, 1963 . . .*"

"I don't care about that," Hill said, his eyes red, shaking his head.

"*Extraordinary courage and heroic effort in the face of maximum danger . . .*"

"Mike, I don't *care* about that. If I had reacted . . . just a little bit quicker. . . and I could've, I guess," Hill said, again, overcome, by the memory. "I'll live with that to my grave."

At the end of the clip, the room was uncomfortably silent.

Reno was clearly moved. "Very powerful, very convincing; *very, very* powerful."

"It wasn't like there was a big debate," Merletti said. "'Gee, you know, it's a close call.' It was overwhelming!"

That evening, Merletti got a call on his White House telephone from Eric Holder. "I don't know how you've done this," Holder told him, "but in the course of twenty-four hours, you have convinced the entire upper echelon of the Justice Department that you're right. You mean to tell me that you gave the same presentation to Ken Starr?" Holder asked.

"Yes!" Merletti said.

"We find it hard to believe that he couldn't see this."

"I'm telling you, Eric, I gave it to him two days ago!"

"Well," the Deputy AG said, "tomorrow you're giving it to him again, and we're coming with you."

The next day, Merletti and Kelleher, along with a contingent of attorneys from DOJ returned to OIC to watch the Secret Service director repeat his entire presentation to Ken Starr.

The attorneys from the department were there to make sure that Starr wasn't cutting the presentation short, that he watched and listened to the same thing. "The people that I met with—over two days," Merletti described, "there had to be at least twenty-five, maybe thirty of them—not one of them believed it until they heard my presentation. After the presentation, I was not aware of anyone who disagreed with me any longer."

In a detailed, twelve-page timeline of the Secret Service matter drafted by OIC, there is no mention of Merletti's second meeting with Starr with DOJ officials present. Although the same memo references

Merletti's first presentation to Starr and Bittman, the timeline does not record any statements made to the director regarding allegations from a source that Merletti facilitated Clinton's relationship with Lewinsky.

After the presentation closed on the *60 Minutes* clip, everyone turned toward Starr for a reaction.

"Mr. Merletti," Starr began, "this office has great respect for the work you and your agents do." He then pulled out a floor plan of the East Wing of the White House. "Now, I'd like you to tell me how agents at the White House are stationed around the family movie theater and what they can see and hear."

Merletti directly looked me in the eye. "In *every* presentation, Starr would get up and say, 'I totally respect Lew Merletti and everything he's done.' There was no respect there. It was all rhetoric. He would say one thing and do another. It was all hypocritical. It was all about politics. It had nothing to do with the truth."

"Janet Reno sat in on one of your presentations and was moved," I said. "Why didn't she just call Starr into her office and say, 'Merletti is making a compelling case—back off?'"

"She did!" Merletti described. "And Starr said, 'I'm not going to.' And that's how we end up in court."

Due to the autonomy required by the Independent Counsel Statute, Reno could only intervene for good cause.

Over the course of Starr's investigation, Merletti received numerous unsolicited messages from law enforcement agencies around the country. Protective agencies from several foreign governments had also contacted him, expressing their concern about Starr's demand for agent testimony. All supported the director's position.

In mid-March, Merletti received a hand-delivered letter from Gary Grindler, deputy assistant attorney general. The Justice Department "has agreed to provide you with legal representation in your official capacity with respect to your upcoming testimony which will be taken in a deposition format by the Office of Independent Counsel for use by a grand jury . . . You should clearly understand," Grindler wrote, "the department does not represent you in your personal capacity . . . you may wish to consider consulting with private counsel."

At his own expense, Merletti hired DC attorney Warren Dennis of Proskauer Rose.

Days later, Merletti received a phone call from former president George H. W. Bush who had been watching news accounts on the issue.

"This isn't right," Bush told him. "You're right. Ken Starr's wrong."

"Don't get involved in this," Merletti warned the man he protected when he served on PPD. "They will drag you through the mud."

"I'm a big boy," Bush said. "I'm getting involved."

At a meeting held at a private residence in Washington, Bush made clear his support of the Secret Service director. "Listen, I appointed Ken Starr. I like the guy, so I'm not going to get into bashing him, but what he's doing is wrong. You *are* going to fight this?"

"That's what I'm involved in," Merletti said. "I'm *in* the fight."

In a speech given by Bush at the Harvard Kennedy School, the former president was asked about Starr's insistence on Secret Service testimony:

[Reporter:] How big a threat to presidential security is the fact that Secret Service agents can now be compelled to testify? And did Kenneth Starr make a mistake in pushing the issue?

Bush: Well, my view differs from the view of many others in my own party, particularly. My view is the Secret Service was right. And I so advised, without anybody asking me to, Lew Merletti, who is the head of the Secret Service. I didn't want it to be interpreted as Starr-bashing because I am not in that mode. I appointed Ken Starr. I respect Ken Starr. I don't like all these orchestrated attacks on Ken Starr. But I know something about the Secret Service, having had Secret Service protection since 1979. I know how they operate. I have never heard one single agent say one single negative thing about any other protectee, someone he or she has been covering. They are nonpolitical.

Citing health concerns, former president Bush declined my request for an interview. However, in a personal letter to Merletti dated April 15, 1998, Bush wrote:

Dear Lew,

I have intended to write you this letter for some time, but today's newspaper coverage regarding the Secret Service's being asked to testify now prompts me to move ahead. . . .

If a President feels that Secret Service agents can be called to testify about what they might have seen or heard, then it is likely that the President will be uncomfortable having the agents nearby. . . . What's at stake here is the confidence of the President in the discretion of the USSS. If that confidence evaporates, the agents, denied proximity, cannot properly protect the President.

Feel free to use this letter with the proper authorities in the special prosecutor's Office, or should the matter go to court, with the proper Officers of the court.

Bush sent a copy of his letter to Ken Starr with a note attached: *"Don't do this. Merletti's right!"*

"It didn't mean a thing," Merletti said. "Not a thing."

8

Weighing the evidence from twenty-five interviews and utilizing the policies and procedures of the Office of Professional Responsibility of the Department of Justice, the Harris Report concluded that no attorney in the Office of Independent Counsel committed professional misconduct.

As to the question of whether Lewinsky was represented by counsel, the investigators found that "under the regulation, a 'represented person' is a person who has retained counsel, where the representation is ongoing and 'concerns the subject matter in question.'"

However, the investigators add, "We find that neither the regulation, its commentary, nor other department materials provide a clear and unambiguous answer to [the] question [of whether Lewinsky was represented by Carter]."

Notwithstanding the legal descriptions, OIC appeared to be skirting ethical lines throughout the events leading up to and during the Lewinsky confrontation. In fact, Michael Emmick, who led the pitch to

Lewinsky, had been an ethics trainer at DOJ, and "consistently urged caution and restraint in considering contacts matters."

Another attorney in the hotel room, Bruce Udolf said in an interview, "It didn't make any difference if Mike had advocated caution; they would have put Bittman in charge of the Lewinsky matter, which is what they did.

"If you look at the end of her report [Harris] says Starr was ill-served by Emmick. I would argue that Emmick was ill-served by Starr, because he was sent in there on a mission, and everybody knew what that mission was going to be. The only thing that Mike and I were concerned about was that the record of that meeting be as clean as possible.

"As it turned out," Udolf added, "that was an impossible task. She was so emotionally distraught and out of control; she alternated between sobbing, screaming, and cursing at the people in the room. I know she described how intimidated she was, and I don't doubt that she was intimidated by the agents and others in the room, but I believe Mike was equally intimidated. I remember thinking, 'I'm glad it's him and not me conducting the interview.'"

In our interview, Harris emphasized that although "the department had no clear and comprehensive regulation, no regulation would resolve the multitude of hard issues or changing circumstances federal prosecutors face in the exercise of their duties. That is why good judgment is paramount."

The report states: "We have found poor judgment in overall stewardship of the confrontation with Lewinsky. By his own admission, Emmick rendered his opinion after a mere 5–10 seconds, having assumed from the beginning that Carter was 'the civil guy, not the criminal guy.'

"There is no question that Lewinsky had an attorney on January 16, 1998. There also can be no doubt that the approach to Lewinsky was entwined with the very subject of her representation by Carter, her potential testimony and affidavit in the Paula Jones case."

Although Harris and Harkenrider recognized "the apparent state of disarray in OIC's Office," they concluded that there *was* time to consider the broader issues.

"This is not the type of analysis and conduct that Starr had a right to expect from his career prosecutors. It exacerbated the public criticism of the Office of Independent Counsel."

Before submitting the report to Janet Reno and Robert Ray, Harris invited Michael Emmick to her New York office to read her findings. "I thought it was the fair thing to do," Harris told me.

After the office visit, Emmick was distraught. "I walked around the streets for hours thinking, if this is released, my career is over."

The report, however, makes one point clear, that Michael Emmick is "a dedicated, talented public servant who, in this one instance, simply did not exercise the good judgment expected of federal prosecutors."

Nevertheless, the analysis and anticipated release of the report were only the beginning of what turned out to be a long, complex subplot worthy of Alfred Hitchcock.

According to DOJ policy, Office of Professional Responsibility (OPR) reports are typically kept within the department unless the case has gained a high level of public attention. Harris said that in such cases, either the full report or a summary is released to the public. The Lewinsky matter was such a case.

In December 2000, Harris submitted a summary to Ray, distilling the narrative, conclusions, and recommendations into twenty-one pages.

However, Ray disagreed with Harris's findings. In an internal memo to Ray from deputy Keith Ausbrook and associate Julie Thomas the two recommended "that you reject the report's finding that Michael Emmick exercised poor judgment." Ray marked the memo "Approved."

Irate, Harris fired off a response.

You guys want to trade on our statements praising OIC for respecting our independence at the same time that you are rewriting our summary and changing our factual determinations, actions which could be read as disrespecting our independence . . .

If you guys really believe that an after-the-fact analysis of what went wrong . . . cannot properly form the basis for a finding of poor judgment . . . we have to wonder what you hired us to do . . .

In Bob's words, when we originally discussed my role and how we would deal with any disagreement: "Put both out there and let the public decide."

For months, Harris and Ray traded summaries to find agreement on special counsels' summary that could be released to the public. Frustrated at finding no middle ground, Harris told Ray to write his own summary.

Sometime during all this back-and-forth, Michael Emmick, disturbed by the report's finding of poor judgment, hired an attorney seeking to have the report sealed by the court.

On May 18, 2001, Robert Ray filed his *Final Report of the Independent Counsel: In Re: Madison Guaranty Savings & Loan Association Regarding Monica Lewinsky and Others*. In the report, Ray abbreviated special counsels' one-hundred-page investigative report and his rebuttal into two and a quarter pages.

Anything submitted to the Special Division is, by statute, sealed. All individuals described in the report are permitted to come to the court, read the section that cites them, and if they choose, submit comments. All comments remain under seal until the Division determines what will be released in a final public document.

After reading Ray's summary at the courthouse, Harris, angered, submitted rebuttal comments to the Division, attaching a copy of her report reiterating her agreement with Ray.

> We discussed what would happen if he did not accept my findings, conclusions, or recommendations. Our shared view was that in such an event, the public interest was so great and public accountability so important that both my findings and conclusions, and his, would be made matters of record, giving members of the public the information needed to form their own views. . . . The independent counsel's description [of the report] is so selective and cursory that it may lead to a misunderstanding of Special Counsel's work product . . .

The Division denied her request.

In a second letter to the court, Harris reiterates her original statements in her first letter. Absent a copy of her report, however, Harris makes clear to the Division about Ray's mischaracterization: "In this response, *we identify certain portions of Appendix C that fail to adequately characterize the SC Report.*"

The Division, again, denied her request.

In a *third* letter to the court, Harris writes:

Both Ms. Harkenrider and I believe it is important to our professional reputations that our comments are included with the independent counsel's mischaracterization of our report . . . or to consider requesting that our names and any mention or description of our Report of Special Counsel be removed from Independent Counsel's Final Report.

Request denied.

The whole matter could have easily been settled had Ray submitted either Harris's full report or her summary along with his rebuttal to the Special Division as a complete package, living up to the agreement he made with Harris at the outset.

During my initial search for her report, I drafted a letter to Merrick Garland, then chief judge of the US Court of Appeals, requesting that the Harris Report be unsealed.

"Judge Garland is recused in the matter," a special assistant responded. "I am forwarding your letter to Judge David B. Sentelle, who was the former presiding judge of the Special Division."

Sentelle's response: "The Special Division no longer exists, and I have no remaining authority over anything connected to that Division."

Harris was incensed.

"*Outrageous!* You can't just say you have no authority and walk away from the matter. You can't have documents sealed, and then say because the Special Division no longer exists that there is no authority to go to regarding unsealing. *Not in this country!*"

At this point, I had successfully uncovered a copy of Harris's full, *unsealed* report in the independent counsel files in the archives.

Before his death in 2015, I contacted Michael Emmick for comment. He explained that his attorney obtained a court order sealing Harris's report and would have her provide me with a copy of the order. When she did not respond, I tracked down her contact information and requested a copy of the order.

No response.

After discussing the issue a couple of times with Robert Reed at the archives, I asked a third time if the Harris Report was under seal. "If the special counsel report prepared by Jo Ann Harris had been marked as under seal, it would not have been released," Reed wrote in an email. "Two other identical copies were located in the independent counsel's records, and neither copy was marked as under seal."

Based on the best available evidence, there appeared to be two scenarios:

1. The counsel for Michael Emmick succeeded in getting an order from the court that prevents Harris, Ray, and DOJ from publishing the special counsel report. Harris said that if such an order exists, she should have received a copy. She never received such an order, and all attempts to obtain a copy from Emmick or his DC attorney were unsuccessful.

2. After Harris submitted her letter requesting that her comments be published in Ray's *Final Report*, the Special Division elected not to publish those comments or her report, as is their privilege, and released the independent counsel's *Final Report* to the public.

In this second scenario, when word reached OIC that Harris's comments and report would remain under seal, Harris believed her report had been sealed from the public.

I asked Harris who at OIC had told her that her report would remain under seal? She recalled that it was either Robert Ray or someone in the office.

"Deliberate or not, Jo Ann, you were misled," I told Harris. "The National Archives did not find any ruling that prohibited the release of your report submitted to Ray and Attorney General Reno. The only copy sealed was the copy you submitted to the Special Division."

She paused for several seconds, "I think you're right, Jim."

When Harris and Harkenrider first discussed how their report would be handled by Ray, Harkenrider remembers asking, "Is this going to be window dressing?"

Harris said that Ray assured her that either the report or her summary would "see the light of day."

"She wouldn't have done it otherwise," Harkenrider confirmed.

A similar scenario played out in 2019, when William Barr, then attorney general, mischaracterized special counsel Robert Mueller's summary of his *Report on the Investigation into Russia's Interference in the 2016 Presidential Election.*

Just as Harris objected to OIC's mischaracterization of her report and wrote three letters to the Special Division requesting that her comments and report be released to the public, Mueller wrote two letters to Barr asking the attorney general to "immediately release the report's introductions and executive summaries," which confirmed that Russia's meddling was calculated to favor Trump's election and that his campaign welcomed their help.

Although Mueller showed that contacts between Russia and Trump operatives had been substantial, he concluded that the evidence did not rise to the level of a criminal conspiracy.

Likewise, although Harris determined that one of Starr's prosecutors exercised poor judgment and made mistakes and that the office developed a plan for discouraging Lewinsky from contacting her attorney, she similarly concluded that their actions did not rise to the level of misconduct. Although the public was able to read a redacted copy of the Mueller Report, the public never heard the full story about the Lewinsky confrontation because the Harris Report remained hidden from the public in the National Archives for 14 years until I uncovered it.

However, there is another facet to the story. Ray's *Final Report* mischaracterizing Harris's findings states:

> The Special Counsel's investigation revealed that there were many others involved in the planning and execution of the encounter, including senior staff of the office . . . and representatives of the Department of Justice, who did not make clear—with opportunities to do so—their specific concerns, if any regarding the proposed contact.

To read Robert Ray's statement, one might infer that Josh Hochberg, the attorney from the Public Integrity section of the department, silently sat on the periphery of meetings as OIC discussed how to approach Lewinsky. In fact, he was fully engaged in the discussion, offering suggestions even as Ken Starr and OIC's senior staff chose not to act on them:

> Hochberg suggested that if OIC had concerns about Carter's reliability, they should serve Lewinsky with a grand jury subpoena which could bring the question of Carter's possible conflict before a court for determination. . . . Hochberg also raised DOJ's regulation regarding contacting a person who

has a lawyer. Hochberg says he told OIC lawyers that if he were they, he would not go forward without first seeking the guidance and protection provided by DOJ through the 'Margolis Procedure'...

Hochberg says that someone, he believes it was Bennett, responded that OIC had looked at the issue of contacting Lewinsky without her lawyer and concluded it was okay. From this response, Hochberg states it was clear to him that OIC did not feel any desire to consult with DOJ on the issue of Lewinsky's lawyer.

While Ray's *Final Report* states that "there were many others involved in the planning and execution of the encounter," Starr and others deferred to Michael Emmick's judgment:

Most of OIC's lawyers with whom we talked, including Emmick, tell us that Emmick was regarded as one of DOJ's top experts on the subject of contacts with represented persons. ... Although all OIC attorneys involved had the obligation to ensure that they were proceeding ethically, they were relying on Emmick to advise them on this issue.

For future such investigations, Harris recommended that the department and office of independent counsel should have more cooperation and complete transparency.

"Every independent counsel office should appoint a PRO [professional responsibility officer]. In other words, someone responsible who would not only be there but be familiar and offer choices such as *Margolis* and spending more time than ten seconds on an issue. I have no problem with one person being totally responsible and available for everyone to come to," Harris told me.

The Office of Independent Counsel has since been replaced by the Office of Special Counsel. Nonetheless, Harris believes the same recommendations should be utilized.

Ken Starr declined several requests for an interview. Robert Ray did not respond. However, former deputies Robert Bittman and Solomon Wisenberg *were* willing to answer questions.

9

Robert J. Bittman was the son of William O. Bittman, a former attorney for DOJ known for successfully prosecuting Teamster boss Jimmy Hoffa. In private practice, he defended E. Howard Hunt Jr., the one-time CIA operative considered the mastermind behind the failed break-in and attempted bugging of Democratic National Committee headquarters at the Watergate Hotel.

The younger Bittman worked as an assistant state attorney in Maryland for six years. Like Ken Starr, Bittman had no experience as a federal prosecutor before he was tapped for Starr's staff in October 1994. He initially served as deputy independent counsel to W. Hickman Ewing in the Little Rock, Arkansas office when the Lewinsky matter broke. He would soon become the head of the Lewinsky investigation when he returned to Washington.

I had questions about both Harris's report and the Secret Service matter.

In our interview, Bittman said he believed the special counsel investigation went beyond what a typical Office of Professional Responsibility investigation would do. "OPR is typically black and white about matters: you violated DOJ policy or DOJ rules or not and [in the Harris Report] they say, [OIC] didn't, or Emmick didn't, but they spent a lot of time criticizing him."

I had several more questions about the report, but he quickly pivoted to a discussion of the Secret Service matter.

However, in his interview with special counsels' Harris and Harkenrider, Bittman said that "Starr's style was to get everyone involved who wanted to be involved. Bittman said it was called 'the deliberative process.'"

In his interview with investigators, Sol Wisenberg labeled, "'The process' . . . an inside joke meaning 'constant meetings, talking things to death.'"

When Bittman was asked who was responsible for spotting whether there was a DOJ policy on an issue, he said that the office was not organized that way. "Rather at meetings, often someone would suggest pulling out DOJ regs on relevant issues. Asked about ethical issues, Bittman said that on borderline ethical issues, 'someone would say, "Call Sam Dash."' . . . [He] added that the office had no 'ombudsman' (such as a Professional Responsibility Officer) to see that DOJ regulations were followed."

But Dash was never contacted before OIC confronted Lewinsky *or* Linda Tripp, and no other independent means of overseeing the ethical issues involved was utilized. However, Wisenberg said, "after the fact, Sam Dash looked at their conduct and 'cleared us on approach night [regarding Tripp.]'"

Dash would later re-examine the issue after learning new information from investigators.

Solomon L. Wisenberg had worked at DOJ under Attorney General Edwin Meese. In 1987, he was appointed an Assistant US Attorney for the Eastern District of North Carolina before moving to Texas as the Chief of the Financial Institution Fraud Unit in the US Attorney's office for the Western District of Texas charged with investigating white-collar crimes. He was introduced to Jackie Bennett, who recruited him as associate independent counsel in 1997. He would become a Starr deputy shortly after the Lewinsky confrontation.

Asked to describe how he would gather information about the Lewinsky matter, Wisenberg told investigators, "I go to the office, open doors where people are meeting and horn in."

This confirmed Harris and Harkenrider's conclusions about the "apparent state of disarray in the office." But they found that "there *was* time to consider the broad issues implicated by the fact that Lewinsky had an attorney."

Wisenberg described the Lewinsky matter as "the case of the century" and said that Emmick had gone "off the reservation" when he offered full immunity to Lewinsky.

After sending him a copy of the report, I began by asking about Sam Dash.

"Ken Starr brought Dash in as an outside, independent, ethics advisor. How often did you or any member of the office consult with him?"

"We consulted with him occasionally," Wisenberg said. "The problem with Sam was that he wasn't around. He was difficult to get ahold of. Sometimes you could reach him; sometimes you couldn't.

There was certainly no process in place where he would automatically be called. And I think his not being called here may have been consistent with the report, [and] Mike [Emmick] not taking the matter as seriously as he should have, not out of any evil or anything, but because he misdiagnosed some of the issues. The office, as a whole, should have thought about this issue more. There's no question."

However, Bittman told special counsels that there *was* a process in place: "on borderline ethical issues, someone would say, 'call Sam Dash.'"

"Were you in the room when Dash was consulting with attorneys?"

"I wasn't a deputy then," Wisenberg said. "I became a deputy very shortly after the Lewinsky thing started, and I was often there when Sam was there. But there were times when Ken met with him alone."

"So, it wasn't part of the process where Dash would meet with the attorneys and enter into the conversation?"

"Sometimes Sam would be there with the whole office. Other times, he would just talk with Ken. He was brought in for what were considered big issues."

"Big issues."

"Yeah."

"But he was never brought in on Lewinsky."

"Well, sure he was."

"Not before the confrontation."

"It sure looks like it, yeah."

"Why didn't anyone check Frank Carter's background?"

"Couldn't really tell you," Wisenberg said. "The report says that some people didn't even know that he did criminal representation, which he obviously did."

"With all the people in the office at that time, I would have thought that that would have been an obvious first step."

"I think that's a fair assessment. Now, if you said Frank Carter, I know him. Not well. He's a civil and white-collar attorney. . . . Most of us on detail were not DC people. Jackie was a DC person. Most of us were not. And if you're not a DC person, you don't know who Frank Carter is. [Bennett] didn't, and [Carter] doesn't have a national reputation. But within DC, he was very well known."

Bennett and Carter did not respond to interview requests.

"Harris says that Lewinsky made clear to Tripp that she had lied to Carter. Why did many at OIC believe that Carter was complicit in Lewinsky's false affidavit? Bittman acknowledges that 'they had information that Lewinsky was misleading Carter,' and Bennett said, 'We didn't know whether Carter was straight or crooked.' Why didn't anyone check Carter's background then?"

"Everybody just assumed, because of the way the Clinton White House worked, and because of our suspicions about [Vernon] Jordan, [advisor to Clinton], and because we didn't know who the hell Carter was, that it was quite possible that he was involved.

"The great fear," Wisenberg stressed, "was that somebody would tip off the president. Nonetheless, we should've known more about Carter.

"On the other hand, you have the compressed time frame. You don't have the online resources that are now available, and you gotta be careful who you call. Somebody might say, 'Well, why are you asking about Frank Carter?'

"But keep in mind," he added, "almost everybody, even before Lewinsky, are lawyered up in this case. But it certainly could have been done, and it certainly *should* have been done."

"On the tapes," I said, "Lewinsky tells Linda Tripp, several times, that she lied to Carter and everyone in the office seems to have ignored that."

"All I can remember about the tapes is that it's not like we got this pristine version of the tapes and everybody sat there and studied them," Wisenberg recalled. "I remember great difficulty with the tapes, and so, things coming out in fits and starts, I had no clear indication that Carter could be involved."

Although Wisenberg was out of town at the time of the Lewinsky confrontation, he offered some thoughts about OIC's decision-making.

"I wasn't in any conversation with [Public Integrity attorney Josh] Hochberg.... I would get most of my information from Jackie [Bennett]. ... The focus was on let's get the tapes, let's stop [*Newsweek* reporter Michael] Isikoff from blowing our cover, and let's get DOJ approval."

"Why didn't anyone take Hochberg's advice about Carter and just serve Lewinsky with a subpoena before a grand jury, which would have taken the issue of complicity out of it?" I asked.

"Well, you would've had to have done it *instanter* [without delay]. What if you give her a subpoena? Do you have a grand jury ready that day? Well, there probably was one. If she's not in custody, do you tell her, 'Meet us at the grand jury?' In other words," Wisenberg said, "how do you get that into a judicial question very quickly? Let's say you convince a judge that Frank Carter has potential conflict. [How do you do that] without Carter being there?"

"Why didn't the office use the *Margolis* procedure as Hochberg suggested?"

"I'd call that pretty fucking good advice, wouldn't you?"

"So why didn't they take it?"

"Beats the hell out of me. I'll bet they wish they had. . . . Now, that doesn't relieve you of your responsibility to make sure you are thinking about those issues."

"I understand the pressure issues, Sol; I'm just surprised that even though Emmick was the expert, and had lectured on ethics, that all of those cautions essentially got thrown out the window because of this great, hot lead."

"Except the ethical rules didn't," Wisenberg countered, "because Mike [Emmick] conformed with the DC ethics rule as interpreted by Judge Norma Holloway Johnson. I would make the important distinction between a governing ethical rule and DOJ regs."

"The point Harris makes several times, is that Lewinsky repeatedly says: 'I want to talk to my attorney'; 'Why can't I talk to Frank?'; 'Why can't Carter represent me in this?' OIC had this preconceived strategy to discourage her from contacting Carter. One of the issues they were concerned with was whether he would contact the White House, and Lewinsky even suggests that they take a taxi over to his office to prevent him from picking up the phone [and calling the White House], and they discouraged that."

"Did anyone else corroborate her on that? She's not a person with high credibility. Neither is Tripp, by the way."

"This credibility issue is interesting, Sol. Individuals seem to be credible when they fit with OIC's plans. When they don't fit with the plan, they're not credible."

"That's classic prosecutor-speak," Wisenberg said.

"Nonetheless, the report confirms that she talked about contacting an attorney several times."

"No, I mean the specific thing about [Lewinsky and prosecutors] driving over [to Carter's office], Wisenberg said.

"That's in the report, Sol."

"What is your question about that?"

"That it crossed an ethical line when she asks for an attorney several times, and they still dissuaded her from contacting Carter and, according to Jo Ann's analysis, offer her a Hobson's choice: talk to us, not Carter, no other choice."

"But Harris doesn't say it crossed an ethical line," Wisenberg stressed. "She says it shows 'poor judgment.' . . . And it doesn't violate the ethical rules of the governing authority."

"Sol, between you and me, wouldn't common sense tell you that if you were the attorney in the room witnessing the confrontation of Lewinsky, and she asks to speak to an attorney multiple times, wouldn't you feel compelled to back off?"

"I can't answer that question because I'm not the same person I was in 1998, because I hadn't been a defense attorney for fifteen years. Under the ethical rules governing DC . . . if federal law enforcement— and that includes agents and prosecutors—are questioning a witness, or questioning even a target, and that target says, 'I want to talk to my attorney,' if that person is not in custody, you can say, 'No, you can't talk to your attorney if you're going to talk to us. You can leave or talk to your attorney.'"

This whole back-and-forth regarding DOJ regulations and ethical rules can sound selective and dense, especially when Wisenberg points out, rightly, that Harris does not directly state that Emmick crossed an ethical line. However, she does make clear in her report "that Emmick was regarded as one of DOJ's top experts on the subject of contacts with represented persons . . . [adding] *all OIC lawyers involved had the obligation to ensure that they were proceeding ethically."*

"The Department of Justice," Harris told me, "made a strong commitment to enforce vigorously the contacts rules when they were in effect; the principles and the related policies involved here remain a vital part of the department's ethical guidelines." Clearly, ethical conduct was Harris's focus in the special counsel report.

However, two individuals with inside knowledge of OIC tell another story regarding the Lewinsky matter.

One source said that Starr was on the phone with other politicians, "especially [Republican Oklahoma governor] Frank Keating, about every other day. He's the lawyer in a major national law firm, the lead prosecutor investigating the president of the United States. Why is he talking to Frank Keating?"

"If Starr was on the phone with him in his office," I asked, "how do you know he was talking to Keating?"

"Because *everybody* knew about it."

"Why was he talking to Keating?"

The source said that it appeared to be "evidence of some political motivation" and labeled the Lewinsky investigation "a political hack job. . . . That whole investigation was never going to be a prosecution of Monica Lewinsky. That grand jury was used to tee up an impeachment trial.

"The grand jury system is supposed to be used to develop evidence of criminal conduct. This was an investigation in search of a crime, or more to the point, in search of grounds for impeachment, and the proof is in the result. That's exactly what happened."

A second source stated, "They made public things that were private in a secret proceeding to embarrass and politically neutralize the president of the United States."

The source described a meeting with several OIC prosecutors where Bruce Udolf abruptly told the group, "Come on—you're gonna impeach this guy over a piece of ass?"

The source pointed to Starr's lack of leadership.

"When you have a leader who sets a tone for the office, and then you wonder why people act in conformity with that tone and then blame *them* for doing what he told them to do, that's not leadership.

"Starr didn't know squat about criminal law," the source candidly said. "People represented by counsel was outside his wheelhouse. He relied on the people pumping him up to go in there and get this thing done [push Lewinsky to flip], and when they did, they're criticized. Mike was doing *exactly* what the people in OIC were encouraging him to do.

"Starr said he was relying on what Mike was telling him [regarding contacts with represented individuals]. While Mike was counseling caution, Starr [and other prosecutors] listened to what they wanted to hear and ignored the rest."

"How did the Lewinsky immunity deal come about?" I asked.

The first source explained that negotiations about immunity took a couple of weeks, that it was difficult dealing with Lewinsky attorney William Ginsburg, a medical malpractice attorney who had represented her father.

"Total blowhard. Had an ego to match his incompetence," the source told me.

Ken Starr's assessment wasn't much better.

"Smart-alecky, Beverly Hills know-it-all. . . . This yahoo cost us a business day."

During a meeting of some forty to fifty attorneys, including Sam Dash, examining the immunity deal brought before them by Emmick and Udolf, Starr and others lashed out at the two because they did not like what they had negotiated.

"Where do you get off offering immunity?" Bennett demanded of Emmick.

"There's no way we should sign this!" another Starr prosecutor added.

Emmick and Udolf were stunned.

Starr looked up from the agreement. "I didn't authorize this."

"Gosh," Emmich politely replied, "I thought I talked about it with other prosecutors there."

Another deputy reacted to the agreement in stark terms: "You guys are the Neville Chamberlain of OIC," a reference to the British prime minister known for his policy of appeasement, in which Chamberlain made allowances to Adolf Hitler hoping to avoid war—a strategy that made Britain look weak.

One of the attorneys who negotiated the agreement maintained that it was made in good faith. "We sent it to him to sign; he signed it," and he refused to go back to Ginsburg and withdraw it.

Two sources confirmed the conversation:

"Ken, I don't know how people here in the Beltway practice, but we sent this document to them to be signed by them. It really doesn't matter if they signed it. It doesn't matter if it was in writing or not.

Where I come from, if you give someone your word, that's it! If you want to withdraw it, fine, but don't ask *me* to do it because I don't feel right about it."

"Well, I'm not going to ask you," Starr said. "I'll have Bob [Bittman] take it over and rescind."

Dash slowly approached the two attorneys at the end of the table. "I appreciate your passion, but we need more from the proffer than what's here."

"Seven months later," the source stated, "and Lewinsky gets a *real* lawyer, Plato Cacheris, and they end up giving her the exact same immunity agreement that they originally declined to honor.

"When I first went to Washington Starr was above reproach, former solicitor general, considered a good guy who replaced Bob Fiske. He was no Fiske."

Starr's ethics advisor, Sam Dash, died in 2004. However, I was able to locate special counsels' interview memo of Dash from May 2000. The memo provides additional insight into Dash's thoughts regarding the Lewinsky confrontation. The document confirms that Dash was never consulted before the brace of Lewinsky. If ever there was a time Starr should have insisted Dash be consulted, this was the time.

After Starr had been attacked in the press, he asked Sam Dash to accept a position as "outside independent expert" regarding ethics and prosecutorial ethics for Starr's office.

Dash explained that he was not a staff member but would check on what was happening at OIC two or three times a week. Although staff attorneys were instructed to contact Dash with issues, he "estimated he may have received about 40 percent of the advice calls that he should have received."

"I was really surprised to hear that he wasn't consulted," Harris told me. "He was very clear that he wasn't."

This appears to differ somewhat from Wisenberg's characterization: "The problem with Sam . . . he was difficult to get ahold of."

"When [Dash] came to the office," investigators describe, "he would ask, 'What happened?' and would often find himself in a reactive, rather than a proactive role. He would try to get all relevant information to determine issues such as the propriety, ethics, and fairness of decisions. Dash said he did not always succeed in getting all the information 'at the time,' 'but [usually succeeded] at some time.' Dash stated that on issues of judgment, he would defer, but on issues involving ethics and legality, he took very strong positions."

In re-examining his work in Starr's office, Dash's observations were stunning. "I saw decisions made on moral grounds that had nothing to do with criminal grounds," Dash told former Clinton communications, public policy advisor, and *Washington Post* reporter, Sidney Blumenthal. "They believed that someone was a bad person, a sinful person, who ought to be punished for it. They distorted their judgment. Ken allowed his personal concepts of morality to interfere with the role of prosecutor.

"One of Starr's problems," Dash told Blumenthal, "was that he had never been a federal prosecutor. He lacked the judgment, even the understanding of the role of a federal prosecutor. So he delegated to these very aggressive prosecutors. Part of my role was to tell him that he was going too far or inappropriate. I said they were not relying on any code of ethics. They wanted to win. They don't have the brakes on them that prosecutors ought to have. His very innocent response was that he was relying on his federal prosecutors."

Dash told Harris and Harkenrider that "he threatened to quit on more than one occasion . . . [and] said he knew nothing about the Tripp and Lewinsky matters until he read about it in the paper and his law school colleagues were pressing for an explanation of what had happened."

Dash quickly went down to the office, where Emmick and Stephen Bates, (a part-time attorney who served as a "scribe" for meetings), described the facts. "At the time, Dash was unaware of any issue relating to Lewinsky's representation. The press stories did not raise this issue; neither did Emmick and Bates. Similarly, the question of offering immunity to a represented person was not raised. Rather, Dash's inquiry on those issues did not take place until October 1998 when [Lewinsky attorney Frank] Carter appeared on the *Larry King Live Show"—nine months* after the Lewinsky confrontation.

Dash recalled the question was raised of whether Lewinsky had been prevented from calling her lawyer. An OIC attorney responded: "What do you mean? We called her lawyer."

"Dash recalled believing that the call was made so that Lewinsky could speak with Frank Carter."

However, the only time OIC reached out to Carter was when Special Agent Fallon called his office and spoke to an answering service without identifying himself. According to Carter, however, if a caller needed to contact him, his answering service had three ways to reach him.

None of the attorneys or Lewinsky spoke with Carter during or after the brace. Before the confrontation ended, Bernard Lewinsky, Monica's father, informed the attorneys by phone that William Ginsburg now represented his daughter, making it unnecessary for prosecutors to speak with Carter.

"Dash also recalled analyzing the contacts question. His analysis was that Carter could not represent Lewinsky in the ongoing crimes of perjury and conspiracy. . . . [Nonetheless, Dash] said to us that this was a dumb strategy and that a good AUSA [Assistant US Attorney] would have told her, 'Get a lawyer.'"

However, when Dash was given additional information from investigators, his judgment became sharper:

Dash was not informed that Lewinsky was told that the value of her cooperation would be less if she called Frank Carter. Nor was Dash informed that Lewinsky was told by agents and/or attorneys that OIC would not tell her attorney as much as they would tell her. Dash never saw the 302s [FBI agents' notes] recounting Lewinsky's desire for the agents to "talk to [my] lawyer." Dash indicated that all of these statements, if made, would have been relevant to his analysis. Dash stated that if he thought "they sought to dissuade her from representation," he would have been very troubled.

Dash had not heard of the possibility that these things had been said to Lewinsky until he heard about them from us. He said that if they sought to dissuade Lewinsky from calling a lawyer, he thought such a strategy could violate Rule 8 relating to misconduct.

Oversight of ethical issues within OIC is important in understanding who was responsible for making such decisions in the office, as special counsels' note:

Starr stated that the office had a designated ethics officer to deal with the Government Ethics Act and matters such as conflicts of interests, receipt of money for outside activities, etc.. As to prosecutorial ethics, the deputies were generally looked to as well as any associate with special expertise on the matter. Additionally, Sam Dash was available for consultation. There was not a specific person designated as a Professional Responsibility Officer or any one person who was to be spotting whether there was applicable DOJ policy on any specific issue [within the office].

If Sam Dash was brought into the office specifically to consult on issues of ethics, why would it be necessary for Starr to look for guidance from his prosecutors at any point, and why wasn't Dash consulted before the office contacted Tripp and Lewinsky?

Michael Emmick appeared to be the only expert in the office who examined the ethical issues related to the Lewinsky brace at the Ritz-Carlton. Sam Dash was out of the loop.

10

What lessons did I draw from Harris and Harkenrider's special counsel report that helped me in understanding the judgment and decision-making of the Office of Independent Counsel regarding the Secret Service matter? Several aspects troubled me:

1. OIC ignored the "Tripp/Lewinsky tapes and Tripp's statements made to FBI agents suggesting that far from participating in the scheme, Carter may have been a victim of Lewinsky's deception. . . . Lewinsky repeatedly made clear to Tripp that she had lied to Carter, stating that you cannot tell your own lawyer the truth if you want him to represent you."

2. OIC appeared to disregard its own attorneys' discussion of the matter. Robert Bittman "acknowledges that they had information from Tripp that Lewinsky was misleading Carter and that there was no real evidence on him." Jackie Bennett said that "they had 'no reason to believe whether Carter was straight or crooked.'"

3. OIC should have checked Carter's background. According to Wisenberg, "Everybody just assumed . . . he was involved." However, "It certainly could have been done, and it certainly *should* have been done."

4. OIC ignored the advice of Josh Hochberg, deputy of the Public Integrity section of the department: (a) that if OIC was concerned that Lewinsky's attorney, Frank Carter, was complicit in lying about knowledge of the relationship between Lewinsky and Clinton, it "should serve Lewinsky with a grand jury subpoena which would bring the question of Carter's possible conflict before a court for determination," and (b) OIC also disregarded Hochberg's suggestion that they take advantage of the *Margolis* procedure, which "was widely promoted throughout the department as a means of getting advice and protection on difficult contacts issues." As investigators point out, David Margolis, associate deputy attorney general, "could be approached to review the facts in sensitive cases and decide whether he personally would 'authorize' the contact to insulate a line attorney from attack. Had they consulted," investigators make clear, "[OIC's] good faith could never have been questioned afterward." As Wisenberg noted, "The office, as a whole, should have thought about this issue more. There's no question."

5. OIC's own FBI agents were unaware of the strategy. "There was no script for the agents' confrontation, but the agents who were 'gaming' by themselves on Thursday night concluded that if Lewinsky asked for her lawyer, he would be contacted, and the confrontation would be lawyer-to-lawyer thereafter."

Harris said that "OIC had no clear playbook in terms of what the agents ought to say."

6. Ethics advisor Sam Dash was brought in by Starr for "big issues," as Wisenberg described. However, Dash was never consulted before the brace of Lewinsky and "was unaware of any issue relating to Lewinsky's representation." Dash said, "One of Starr's problems was that he had never been a federal prosecutor. He lacked the judgment and even the understanding of the role of a federal prosecutor." Dash told investigators that he "knew nothing about the Tripp and Lewinsky matter until he read about it in the paper." Dash said that "if [OIC attorneys] sought to dissuade Lewinsky from calling a lawyer, he would have been very troubled."

7. Based on the best available evidence, Robert Ray appears to have broken his agreement with Harris regarding the way they would deal with any disagreement concerning her report. As Harris described to OIC attorneys in a memo and letters to the Special Division, Ray stated that they would "put both reports out there [the special counsel report or summary and Ray's rebuttal] and let the public decide." This is further evidenced by the fact that Ray challenged draft after draft of Harris's summary for months. Second, Harris appears to have been misled into believing that when the Special Division sealed a copy of her report attached to her second letter, the Division had sealed her report from the public, when in fact, the Division *only* sealed what was submitted by Harris to the Division, not her original report submitted to Ray and Reno. Although this may well have been unintentional, it could

possibly be interpreted that OIC was acting to protect one of its attorneys.

There were two driving factors in OIC's handling of the Lewinsky confrontation. The first was Ken Starr's belief that Carter was complicit in Lewinsky's effort to lie. "The way in which Lewinsky ended up with Carter caused some of OIC staff to have suspicions that Carter was complicit in the scheme. . . . This was so because, in Starr's words, it was their '*instinct* based upon experience with the Clinton people.'" But, as the report states, "there was little evidentiary basis for concluding that Carter was involved in any scheme to commit perjury."

The second factor was Michael Emmick's "general overconfidence in his own expertise." Moreover, he was pressured, according to a source. "While Mike was counseling caution, Starr [and other prosecutors] listened to what they wanted to hear and ignored the rest. Mike was doing exactly what the people in OIC were encouraging him to do."

All these errors in judgment and decision-making, led by a man with no experience as a federal prosecutor, along with a covert source inside the Secret Service feeding them uncorroborated information, resulted in OIC pursuing Director Merletti as a possible co-conspirator whose mission, OIC believed, was calculated to protect the president.

Although Bill Clinton was ultimately responsible for the Lewinsky matter, the facts strongly suggest that OIC was willing to do whatever it took to get Clinton.

Between September and November 2014, I exchanged emails and phone calls with Michael Emmick. Because of his work as a Los Angeles–based attorney and teacher at Loyola Law School, it was difficult for him to schedule time to discuss the issues. In one conversation, however,

I asked if he had any regrets about his involvement in the Lewinsky confrontation.

His voice slowed. "I regret a great deal," and with hindsight, would have "handled it differently."

He then disclosed that he had been diagnosed with a brain tumor and was going in for surgery and that we would talk in a week.

In what turned out to be a final email, he wrote, "The world is often much more complex than outsiders can readily discern. We'll talk later, Mike."

Over the next weeks and months, I tried to reach him. Eventually, I learned that although his surgery had been successful, he was walking on the beach near his home when he suffered a fatal heart attack.

Around this same time, I received an email from Jo Ann Harris apologizing for missing our appointment to talk.

"Health took a dive," she wrote. "Call when you have a moment."

Although that was the last email I received from Harris, it was not the last phone conversation we had. At one point, she confided that the lung cancer that had been removed had now spread and that she was due to go into the hospital for more treatment. By this time, I had been in contact with her for three years and had gained her trust. Before going into the hospital, she gave me her cell number and told me to call with any additional questions. During a final conversation, I could tell she was worn out.

"Jo Ann, you sound tired. Let's pick up in a couple of days."

"*No,*" she firmly said. "I may not be here in a couple of days. Let's finish it now."

Harris died a week later.

In one of our earliest conversations, however, she offered additional thoughts on the Lewinsky matter. One thing she repeated was that the upper echelon at DOJ believed the entire Lewinsky investigation was a complete waste of time by Starr.

Harris's own opinion was sharper: "I don't think we ought to be investigating crap like this."

I told Harris that I was surprised to learn that no one attempted to find out who Carter was before approaching Lewinsky.

"It really forms the basis of my judgments, that they didn't care whether he was complicit or not. [Carter] would have had an obligation to correct what he had participated in, which is the false affidavit, and it would have blown the whole chance to get Lewinsky and Clinton."

Harris was particularly indignant about the replacement of veteran prosecutor Robert Fiske with Ken Starr.

"Did the Special Division offer any reasons why they were replacing Fiske?"

"Nope," she said with obvious irritation.

"Did they give any reasons why they were appointing Starr?"

"Nope. I was stunned."

"Were you with the department at the time?"

"Yes," Harris said. "I think they [the Special Division] took the only professional prosecutor I have ever known to investigate something as important as this and took him off the case and appointed a judge."

"Was there legal precedent for replacing Fiske?"

"I don't think that this particular set of circumstances had ever arisen before," Harris said. "It never dawned on us that they would replace Fiske. He had a huge staff. I mean, he was bumping right along, and he's a pro. I have been on independent counsel staffs myself, and [I] just wondered what on earth the court was doing appointing judges to a prosecutor's office. We had a perfectly good [regulatory] independent counsel in Bob Fiske, a professional prosecutor ... very straight-forward, nonpolitical—just a good guy.

"What really happened," Harris explained, "is that the Independent Counsel Statute had expired and was heading for renewal. Janet Reno appointed Bob Fiske, and then the statute kicked back in, again empowering the court to appoint an independent counsel. And the department said, 'Keep Fiske. He's well into his investigation.' And the Special Division, instead, appointed Ken Starr."

Seven months into his investigation, the reasoning used in replacing Fiske was that he had been appointed by Reno, a Clinton appointee and the Division opted to avoid the appearance of bias. If that's true, why didn't they appoint another experienced federal prosecutor instead of a judge who lacked such skills?

In fact, as Starr writes in his memoir about his first meeting with Robert Fiske: "Fiske's sweeping investigative focus—financial chicanery, political fund-raising hijinks, and dubious real estate transactions—was nowhere near my professional sweet spot."

Acknowledging his lack of experience, why didn't Ken Starr simply go back to the Division and withdraw as independent counsel before beginning his work?

"Fiske was a friend of yours," I said to Harris. "Did you have a conversation with him after he was dropped?"

"I'm the one who *told* him he was dropped," Harris said.

"What was his reaction?"

"I got him when he got off an airplane, and his words were, 'You have *got* to be kidding!' But he's a pro. I don't think he ever went public about his feelings."

"Do you think the decision was political?"

"Yup."

11

During the more than three hours I spent with Merletti, he shared dozens of documents from his files as director, including an edited copy of the PowerPoint presentation he gave to Starr and DOJ officials, as well as letters from both Monica Lewinsky and former president George H. W. Bush.

"Let me back up a minute," Merletti said.

"Once I meet with Ken Starr—and I'm telling you, I might as well have been talking to the wall—I had a very good presentation. It was about life and death. It was about the United States of America, the office of the Presidency, and what the Secret Service is about. We are there for continuity of government.

"We dress as soldiers, doctors, engineers, graduates," Merletti said as he took me through a printout of his presentation. "This shows us as umpires. Here I am at a ballgame. This is an agent dressed as a chauffeur, a priest with the pope."

Throughout it all, Merletti repeatedly emphasized the critical need for proximity.

"This letter is addressed to Senator Kerry," Merletti said, handing me a letter sent to then-senator John Kerry from Secret Service director John Magaw:

> We are gravely concerned about the action you and the Select Committee are about to take with respect to a former employee, John Syphrit. Mr. Syphrit was part of the Secret Service for nearly a decade, and during that time, participated in the protective security afforded to President Reagan and then Vice President Bush. As a consequence of his assignment and the duties he performed, Mr. Syphrit may have been in a position to overhear some conversations and discussions in which they participated. The Select Committee has recently subpoenaed Mr. Syphrit in order to compel his testimony regarding at least one possible conversation which he purportedly overhead during the scope of his employment.
>
> Mr. Chairman, let me say at the outset that we do not challenge the Select Committee's authority to issue such a subpoena nor dismiss the important issue which you are investigating. We do, however, strongly object to the issuance of the subpoena in these circumstances. No Secret Service employee has ever been required to disclose information he or she may have overhead by virtue of a protective assignment. To compel an employee or former employee of the Secret Service to reveal such a conversation would violate the trust and confidence which is the foundation of our ability to perform our mission.
> . . .
> Mr. Chairman, this is not a partisan or political issue for the Secret Service. The Secret Service serves and protects men and

women from both parties and various countries. Many of your fellow Senators can attest not only to the professionalism of the Secret Service, but also to their confidence and trust in its employees. They will also tell you how important it was for them to be able to speak freely and candidly while our agents were in close proximity to them and their closest advisors. Before the Select Committee takes this step we would ask that you consult with those Senators who have received Secret Service protection. . . .

I am personally and genuinely concerned about the detrimental impact this action will have on the Secret Service's future ability to protect our nation's leaders, candidates and honored guests. Those under our protection could be forced to curtail their conversations and could force us to alter our protective methods and pose serious security concerns.

"They pulled their subpoena back *immediately*," Merletti said, snapping his fingers. "'We're absolutely not doing this,' they said."

"Was that in your presentation to Starr?"

"Yeah. Oh, Starr couldn't care less. I'm telling you, everything I'm showing you, he saw and probably five times more. I had a presentation that went two and a half hours, maybe closer to three."

Merletti then talked about a call he received at his home late one night.

"Lew?" a voice said softly.

Merletti recognized the voice of a confidant, but before he could acknowledge with a name, the friend interrupted.

"I'm calling from an unsecured outside line. Look, I've been following your battle with Ken Starr. We all have. I know you're acting on principle, but . . ."

"But what?" Merletti asked.

The caller paused. "You need to know something . . ."

"Know what?"

"Lew," the friend advised quietly but firmly, "there are those who want to take the president down. They perceive that you are in their way, and they will destroy you now and in the future. My advice to you is to get the best attorney you can afford, and don't call me until this is over."

Merletti said the call was made in strict confidence from a longtime friend. "This is an individual I trust, and [they're] warning me."

Despite fears of retaliation, Merletti believed he had to move forward. With the help of Justice officials, Merletti and Kelleher went to court. They lost in DC district court and appellate court.

"We go in front of two judges," Merletti said, "and all they're looking at is, literally, the letter of the law. That's it! They don't understand protection. They don't understand assassination. And Ken Starr has no idea about this either. He doesn't care about it. He wants to win this thing, and he's going to walk away and leave the Secret Service with a big mess on their hands."

In early July, Merletti and Kelleher met with Seth Waxman, solicitor general, the attorney who represents the federal government before the US Supreme Court.

"I'm called over to the Justice Department, and I'll never forget this. We go in, big conference room, me and Kelleher, and about eight—maybe more—attorneys and Waxman walk in. 'We're not taking this to the Supreme Court,' Waxman says. 'We lost in district court; we lost in appellate court. We're done.'"

"OK," I interrupted, "tell me again exactly what you lost—that you could refuse to testify?"

"Correct. That we wanted this privilege to *not* testify."

What the Secret Service was seeking, what DOJ was fighting for, was a "protective function" privilege similar to doctor–patient and attorney–client confidentiality. Because of the proximity necessary between agents and protectees, they argued, any conversation agents overhear of the president should remain confidential, and as with doctor–patient and attorney–client relationships, they should not be compelled to reveal such conversations to a grand jury or court of law. The one exception is if an agent observed a criminal act.

"If we saw a crime," Merletti stressed, "you wouldn't have to ask us. We'd report it. I would have been the agent in charge of the president's detail. I would have gone to my director; I would have gone to the secretary of the Treasury. But we hadn't witnessed a crime!

"We are a dedicated, tactical organization. There's no organization in the world that does what we do. And we believe that our skills are perishable. So, we must constantly work at them, constantly, *constantly* work at them. In one Division of the president's detail, we had to shoot a thousand rounds a month.

"Now, we've got this guy, Ken Starr, asking us, 'Was that woman's lipstick on straight?' You think we're looking at someone's lipstick? We're looking for terrorists. Bin Laden was on our radar. We're ready at any moment to respond, and you want us to watch women's lipstick and hair?

"Agents are posted around the Oval Office," Merletti described, "however, number one, you can't see inside; number two, you can't see the other post. You don't know who's in there, and you don't care, as long as they walk by and have a badge with the right encryption on it. That's all you care about."

Although Merletti appreciated Waxman's professionalism, he was not prepared to give up the fight.

"If you give up," he told the solicitor general, "I will go to the American people. I will not let the men and women in the Secret Service who have vowed to give their life to save the life of the president of the United States . . . I will not let them down. If they're willing to fight that way, you think I'm going to back down? We're going to fight and fight and *fight!*"

With that, Merletti and Kelleher left the room. But before they could reach the end of the hall, an attorney called them back. "OK, you've convinced Waxman. We'll go to the Supreme Court."

Waxman was unable to recall any additional information.

While the fight was working its way to an outcome in the Supreme Court, Merletti said that more than one member of Congress approached him. "Cooperate with Starr," they said, "and we'll *give* you the privilege you're seeking."

In fact, on August 13, four days before Clinton's grand jury testimony, Merletti received a fax of draft legislation from the Senate Judiciary Committee for a yet-to-be-numbered Senate bill proposed by Vermont senator Patrick Leahy. Among the bill's details were the following:

(5) Secret Service personnel must remain at the protectee's side on occasions of confidential and intimate conversations and,

as a result, may overhear top-secret discussions, diplomatic exchanges, sensitive conversations, and matters of personal privacy.

(6) The necessary level of proximity can be maintained only in an atmosphere of complete trust and confidence between the protectee and his protectors.

(7) If a protectee has reason to doubt the confidentiality of actions or conversations taken in sight or hearing of Secret Service personnel, he might seek to push the protective envelope away or undermine it to the point where it could no longer be fully effective.

The bill also addressed issues of possible criminality:

(11) Because Secret Service personnel retain law enforcement responsibility even while engaged in their protective function, the privilege must give way concerning information that, at the time it was acquired, was sufficient to provide reasonable grounds for believing that a crime had been, was being, or would be committed.

But the legislation went nowhere.

12

Of all the interviews I conducted for the Merletti story, the most problematic was that of deputy independent counsel Robert Bittman. Although I had a list of questions concerning the Harris report, he briefly stated his critique and quickly moved on to Merletti.

"You wrote several praising things about Merletti," Bittman said, having read a profile I had written about the Secret Service director on my website.

"I interviewed him, yes."

"I think he made a huge mistake that hurt the Secret Service and will continue to hurt them forever."

"I want to get all perspectives, Bob."

"Let's talk about Merletti. I have high respect for the work that the Secret Service does. We were faced with an allegation that the president made in his deposition, the statement regarding his contacts with Lewinsky. Many of the statements he made under oath could be proven true or not true by the Secret Service. We requested to talk to them, and they said 'No,' and Merletti came in with me, Ken, and one other guy from our office and made a presentation about why they thought it was necessary that they not be required to speak to us about these things.

"We went through what we wanted to talk about and why," Bittman said. "Our initial request was to determine whom we would talk to, records, specific times, who was on duty, and initially, they didn't want to give us those records at all.

In our initial interview, Merletti said that he immediately supplied Starr's office with all White House access records on Monica Lewinsky: E-Pass, Movement and Waves.

"Merletti made a very compelling presentation about why they did not want to talk to us. They discussed previous assassinations, not of US presidents, but other political figures and why it was necessary for the protectee to have confidence in the Secret Service, and I think there was a Secret Service lawyer there that believed that the Secret Service was [exempt from testifying] by a 'protective function' privilege, even though it has never been recognized."

While Bittman's recollection matched Merletti's regarding the attendance of Secret Service chief counsel John Kelleher, his memory about the presentation differed from what Merletti shared with me. The edited, printed PowerPoint presentation I was shown in Merletti's office detailed multiple assassinations and attempts on previous US presidents, as well as protective tasks for foreign leaders, a portion of the same presentation he gave to department officials and Janet Reno.

"We told them," Bittman said, "that there is no way the court will recognize this privilege. Let's work this out. We don't want to intrude on the Secret Service mission and [will] do everything in our power to completely limit the information we need."

Bittman described months and months of meeting DOJ and Treasury officials.

In a "Talking Points" memo prepared for a March 29, 1998 meeting to discuss the privilege, Starr's office laid out several points:

This privilege does not exist. There is no legal authority for it, whatsoever. . . . [it] appears to be very conveniently tailored to prevent us from obtaining any information that might incriminate the president.

While there is no legal standing on the privilege, the importance of confidentiality is not only stated in the commission book for agents but had been repeatedly stressed by previous directors and honored in the past by Senate committees, a point Merletti made in all his presentations.

The memo:

Secret Service agents and uniformed officers have testified on numerous occasions in the past . . . John Hinckley's trial, the Warren Commission proceedings, 'Squeaky' Fromme.

All those examples concerned criminal matters that were a necessary exception, as Merletti stated in all his presentations.

The memo:

Even if the "protective function" privilege does exist, it must at least be subject to the exception recognized in *US v. Nixon*, (418 US 683) in 1974. Thus, claims of a privilege based only on a "generalized interest in confidentiality" must yield to the "fundamental and comprehensive" need to develop facts in a criminal investigation. (Id.at 709, 713).

Bittman is likely referencing Watergate, where Secret Service agents were asked to testify regarding what they may have heard on tape recordings made of President Richard Nixon's Oval Office conversations. Although the Secret Service had installed and maintained the recording system, "under no circumstances are any tapes monitored by representatives from this service," Louis Sims, the special agent in charge of the USSS Technical Security Division, wrote in a memo at the time. Sims told me that although he did testify before Judge John Sirica, his testimony *only* described the purchase of a tape recorder used by Nixon secretary, Rosemary Woods enabling the transcription of the Oval Office tapes. As to the question of whether other agents testified about conversations by Nixon, either recorded or overheard, Sims stated that it "never happened to my knowledge."

The memo:

The claim that the privilege extends to hearsay communications is ridiculous.

Confidentiality extends to *all* conversations an agent overhears regarding a protectee, including hearsay.

"Even if OIC recognized the privilege," Bittman explained in our interview, "the White House said that the privilege is held by the Treasury and/or protectee.

"We asked for a waiver. Can't do it because Treasury holds the privilege. 'Why not ask the protectee if he will waive the privilege?' 'No, we're not going to even ask him,' they said. Clearly, we were being stonewalled. We tried to work things out. 'We don't need agents' actual testimony; we don't need to talk to people that didn't even see anything.' They wouldn't even work with us to identify people through a questionnaire.

"'We don't need to know names, just answer questions, and we will then discuss.' They steadfastly refused. We said, 'If you force us to litigate, you will lose because there is no basis in law.' And we never lost. We were thirteen to zero.

"'It would be worse for the Secret Service if you litigate and lose your privilege than to give us some moderate stuff,' Bittman told Treasury and DOJ officials. "They refused. The DC circuit and Supreme Court said that there was no 'protective function' privilege. The way they handled it was very disappointing."

In one meeting, Bittman described, "Ken Starr said, 'Are you telling me that if a Secret Service officer overhead Nixon instructing someone to destroy the Watergate tapes that that person should not have to come forward?' And they said, 'Yes,' and Starr said, 'I disagree.'"

Actually, as Starr recorded in his handwritten notes from April: "If a Secret Service agent saw RN [Richard Nixon] burning the tapes . . ."

If such a scenario took place, I reasoned, would agents identify this as a crime? More accurately, if they saw Nixon erasing tapes, would that be a reportable crime? And if agents did not monitor the tapes, how would they conclude that it might be a crime to destroy them?

"I don't know Merletti to be a bad guy," Bittman said. "I think he received information that he was specifically instructed not to go into but was pressured to make sure that no people talked."

"Can you explain about a tip that came from inside the Secret Service that alleged that Merletti struck a deal with Clinton? Starr brought this up at your first meeting with the director."

"Was it at that meeting with the presentation? I don't remember that, but it was known throughout the office."

"Where did the tip come from?"

"I didn't get tips."

"But you were the head of the entire Lewinsky investigation."

"Right, but I didn't get all the tips. Tips didn't come to me. I don't remember if it was a member of the media or somebody else."

"Was an effort made to check the credibility of the tip?"

"Yes. We did take steps to verify, but it was a private conversation between the president and Merletti and relayed to somebody else that got back to us.

"Merletti told someone at the Secret Service," Bittman described, "and that person whom he told, 'Joe Smith,' told someone else who was not in the Secret Service, and that someone told us. I don't remember if we spoke to 'Joe Smith' or not."

"So, the tip came from someone *outside* the Secret Service who had heard from someone *inside* the Secret Service, correct?"

"Correct. We did talk to Merletti. Merletti always agreed to talk to us, but he denied it."

"What can you tell me about a Sunday afternoon meeting at the department with Janet Reno and Eric Holder to discuss the privilege?"

"I was probably there. I don't remember. I know that I worked with one of Holder's deputies, Jonathan . . ."

"Schwartz?" I volunteered.

"Jonathan and I got along very well. We tried to resolve this. We came to several different agreements, all of which were shot down by Treasury or the White House because DOJ was negotiating on behalf of Treasury."

"What happened with your discussions with Schwartz after that Sunday meeting?"

"We tried several things—waiver, questionnaire—and Jonathan, a former prosecutor, knew what we couldn't agree to and what made sense."

As an example, Bittman described, "If they came back and said, 'OK, we've talked to our people, and they don't know anything.' Jonathan knew that that couldn't be acceptable to us."

"Reno and Holder shared the opinion that Merletti's stand on protection was principle based, not political, and you're saying that you disagreed with that?"

"Yes. What they were saying was that they needed this 'protective function' privilege so that they can better protect presidents in the future, and we said, 'We don't disagree, as a general principle. However, there should be exceptions, and this was one of them.'

"We offered to protect whatever information they provided, apart from everything else, super-grand-jury protection that would never become public, which was one of the things they feared. I said, 'If you litigate with us and lose, you risk agents being videotaped walking into the grand jury, so how is that helping your cause?' The department ultimately decided to litigate. Was that a principled decision? I'm more inclined to think that it would have been on Reno's part than Holder's."

In a letter from Jackie Bennett to Eric Holder, Bennett writes, "*We have bent over backwards to accommodate the Secret Service's concerns in our questioning of its personnel. . . . What happened yesterday was, in my view, an effort by sworn officials of the Executive Branch to hinder this investigation.*"

Holder did not respond to multiple interview requests.

"However, you did depose agents," I told Bittman.

"We tried, yeah."

"No, you *did* depose agents. I'm looking at a list in front of me."

"We tried in that we did conduct them. The people who handled this on the part of DOJ were obstructionists, and that was recognized in the department, and it didn't work," he said. "I conducted some of those and suspect those are public now, right?"

"I found some of them on C-SPAN. In watching the agents' testimony, they all seem consistent in that they had no knowledge that they ever saw or heard anything."

"That's very possible. Very possible that we didn't have the right people in there. I never thought there was any Secret Service agent who saw Lewinsky and the president engaging in a sex act. We were willing not to talk to every agent."

"Well, you spoke to thirty-three agents, including Merletti."

"That's right," Bittman said. "I think, even after we won, we offered them to be interviewed rather than go to the grand jury, and they said, 'No.'"

"Are you aware of a conversation Ken Starr had with Merletti where Starr claims—through another tip or the same tip—that when Merletti was head of PPD, that he facilitated the Clinton/Lewinsky relationship by removing him from the White House, putting him in the back seat of a car, covering him with a blanket, and taking him to a hotel to meet Lewinsky?"

"What's your question: Was I aware of the tip or that Ken told Merletti?"

"Both," I said.

"I was not aware that Ken told Merletti, but I'm aware of the allegation."

"And how did that end up?"

"I don't know. I don't remember if it was the same source."

This is another bit of confusion regarding Bittman's recollection. Earlier, he confirmed attending Merletti's presentation: "Merletti made a very compelling presentation about why they did not want to talk to us."

According to Merletti's account someone at that meeting said, "We have information that *you*, Mr. Merletti, were involved in putting the president in the back seat of a car, covering him with a blanket, taking him out of a White House context, taking him to a hotel, getting Monica Lewinsky there, and allowing them to be alone in a room."

Bittman apparently did not attend the meeting where this conversation occurred.

Merletti confirmed that the "blanket" allegation took place at his first presentation to Starr and Bittman at OIC offices.

Continuing, I read a piece from *Truth at Any Cost*: "[OIC] gave up when their informant, whom they assured of confidentiality, refused to go on the record."

"Were you aware of that?"

"Aware of what?"

"That OIC tried to get the source to go on the record?"

"That rings a bell."

"This is not the secondhand source who gave you the tip, but the *actual* source inside the Secret Service."

"I'm not sure. Several things about tips, we would get several tips on a big case, and some are crazy."

In an interview, Sol Wisenberg confirmed that the office received "a lot of nut calls."

"Some won't go on the record," Bittman recalled. "I do remember that this was one of them."

"I imagine that a tip coming from someone inside the Secret Service would be substantially more important than others, would it not?"

"Yes," Bittman said.

"Did this person, who alleged direct knowledge of Merletti facilitating the Clinton/Lewinsky relationship, ever come to the office and speak to you and Ken?"

"I don't remember. My memory is that I never directly received this tip, but I would have been made aware of details of the source and would have been involved in discussions about how we track it down. I don't remember Ken talking to Merletti about it."

"I spoke with Sol Wisenberg. When the tip from Linda Tripp came into the office, prosecutors went out to her house that night to interview her. If they did that for Tripp to determine credibility, why didn't you and Ken meet with the source inside the Secret Service?"

"The source never wanted to meet. My memory is that the source came to Jackie [Bennett]. To the extent that you quote me, you should say that I'm not positive of any of this, but that's why I have a vague recollection that the source may have come in through the media or been in the media or something like that."

"I would think that if you had a source inside the Secret Service offering information that would help your investigation, even if the tip came to Jackie, you would want to interview this individual to check his legitimacy."

"I agree with that, generally, but I don't think that person wanted to formalize whatever the information was. I thought I remembered that Jackie did go back and talk to the person. Someone was able to get more information, but if the person had been willing to sit for an interview and formalize his or her allegations, we would have done that."

"So, you're saying it never got to that point?"

"I don't think so, yes."

"And the only contact the tip had with OIC, based on your memory, was with Jackie Bennett?"

"Yes, but I don't have a strong recollection. He would know better than me."

Bennett did not respond to multiple requests for an interview.

For the March 29 meeting discussing the privilege, an OIC "Talking Points" memo reports, "We have specific and credible information regarding statements by the President to Director Merletti that may constitute obstruction of justice."

The memo may be referencing an event that took place earlier that month. Jackie Bennett met with retired NBC producer Ira Silverman, who was asked by Tim Russert, NBC Washington bureau chief at the time, to investigate the Secret Service/Lewinsky connection.

Silverman reported that a source had attended a conference at Secret Service headquarters. According to Silverman, the source alleged that "he overheard a hallway conversation where President Clinton summoned Merletti to the White House (around January 4 or 5) and said, 'I don't want to hear anything coming from any Secret Service agents about girls in the Oval Office.' According to the source, John Kelleher, chief counsel, said that Merletti had received "a finger in the chest, from the president, for emphasis."

Merletti denied any such conversation with the president, and I did not locate any document in OIC files to substantiate the claim of such a White House meeting.

I contacted John Kelleher to comment.

"That would be a negative," Kelleher said in a phone conversation. "I don't talk about anything to do with the Secret Service."

Former President Clinton declined an interview request.

Returning to my interview with Bittman, I asked, "Were you present during the Holloway-Johnson hearing?"

"Yes."

"What was that like?"

"She was very skeptical of the privilege. Based on other litigation and other conversations we had with her, she pretty much formed in her mind that the White House was virtually doing everything they could to prevent us from getting information. That's my memory."

"What I don't understand," I said, "is how Judge Susan Webber Wright sided with the Secret Service in the Paula Jones matter."

"I don't think that's right," Bittman said, "about what Webber Wright ruled on. We never had an adverse judgment on the Secret Service. She did not rule on the Secret Service issue. She ruled in our favor regarding communication in the White House, which was a separate issue during the Lewinsky thing. The Supreme court denied the 'protective function,' but I don't remember Wright ruling on Secret Service issues, but I could be mistaken."

Webber Wright had ruled that four Secret Service agents did *not* have to testify in the Paula Jones matter.

I read a passage to Bittman from Ken Gormley's book, *Death of American Virtue*:

> In January, Paula Jones's lawyers had tried to subpoena four Secret Service agents in close proximity to the president. . . . Judge Webber Wright had slammed the door shut on this inquiry, ruling that US Secret Service agents' observations had no bearing on 'the core issues in this case.' The judge wrote, there existed a real possibility that interrogating these agents could 'provide critical information at the core of how the Secret Service actually functions,' which could create an 'unacceptable' risk to the president and others if disclosed.

"And you're saying that she ruled in your favor?"

Actually, *I'm* wrong here. The ruling was against Paula Jones's personal attorneys, *not* Starr prosecutors. However, the unacceptable risk point Webber Wright was making was the core of Director Merletti's argument.

"No. Look," Bittman said, "you're not understanding what I'm saying. I never said that. I don't remember that ruling. That's what I said."

I wanted to go back and reread the passage to try to understand Bittman's point but was cut off.

"You know, maybe we ought to stop talking. Thank you."

13

On Friday, July 17, 1998, a few minutes before noon, William Rehnquist, US Supreme Court chief justice, issued his decision denying a stay in testimony from Secret Service agents. No sooner had he announced his decision, OIC immediately issued subpoenas, and three Secret Service agents appeared before a grand jury that afternoon.

Among the agents subpoenaed was Larry Cockell, then current special agent in charge of Clinton's protective detail.

"Cockell wasn't even *on* [the president's protective detail] when the entire Monica Lewinsky episode took place," Merletti noted. "Cockell was so distracted by the subpoena—the media was camped outside his home and followed his son to school—that he came to my office and said that he felt he should step down until he could refocus on our mission. Cockell was a great agent; he was a man of integrity." This was "the final motion of disrespect [by Starr]," Merletti said.

Although the legal battle may have ended, and testimony from agents had begun, Merletti's story took another turn. After Starr finally secured an immunity deal that kept Lewinsky in the clear, OIC took possession of her semen-stained, blue dress and turned it over to the FBI. When Starr notified Louis Freeh of his plans to test Clinton's blood, the FBI Director was stunned.

"Wait a minute," Freeh told Starr, "This is ridiculous. We're talking about taking a DNA sample from the president of the United States to compare with semen on a dress? This is like a bad movie."

Nonetheless, a blood sample was obtained from Clinton, and forensic testing began.

After considerable stalling, Clinton finally agreed to testify before a grand jury on August 17. Earlier that month, however, another drama played out in a scheme involving intentionally false information.

Approximately five-hundred people were attending a black-tie dinner of the Marine Corps Law Enforcement Foundation (MCLEF) in Atlantic City, New Jersey. The annual event raises money for the families of fallen law enforcement officers. Among those in attendance that evening were Merletti and another man who approached the director's table during an intermission. FBI special agent, Tom Pickard, wanted a word. Working with OIC, Pickard was the assistant director of the FBI's Criminal Investigative Division.

"Have a seat," Merletti told him. "We can talk here."

"No, no," Pickard said, "this really needs to be in private."

"I get up," Merletti recalled, "and he's leading me. We're moving between tables, and out into the lobby. We pass people smoking cigars as he takes me to a secluded area, where we sit on a couch."

Pickard began by sympathizing with the director before quietly offering some alleged inside information. "I know it's been a tough time for you and the Secret Service. I'm in charge of the lab that's testing the dress." He paused, letting the information sink in. "That dress . . . is *clean*. It was either a new dress or she had it dry-cleaned, but Lew . . . there's *no* DNA on that dress."

Ken Starr's notes from July, a few weeks before the conference, reference "FBI lab work" and "Tom Pickard."

The two remained seated for a moment longer before Pickard got up and disappeared into the evening's event.

Merletti remained on the couch for a few more minutes. "What's this all about?"

Merletti reasoned that Starr was looking to see if he would tip off the president before his grand jury appearance to further incriminate Clinton. Starr and his FBI agents were still trying to validate their Deep Throat source claiming Merletti's close relationship with Clinton. The source had since declined to go on the record.

In researching Merletti's account of the Pickard exchange, I contacted MCLEF. I spent the better part of an afternoon trying to pin down the exact date of the black-tie event he described.

The important detail was the date when the dinner was held. Merletti believed it was August 3, 1998, fourteen days before Clinton's grand jury testimony with OIC prosecutors meeting at the White House. A representative from the organization disputed Merletti's recollection. However, he referred me to an individual who had not only worked for MCLEF but was the co-chair of the event in 1998. At first, he said that Merletti's date was off by a couple of months. Then he backtracked, remembering that the hotel where the event was held was undergoing renovations that year, and determined that Merletti's memory was off by *two days* of the actual event, held on Saturday, August 1. This was later confirmed when I asked Merletti's associate, Kat Mathis, to check his calendars during his tenure as director.

Nonetheless, Merletti strongly denied Starr's claim that there was any deal between himself and Clinton. As he made clear to me, "[Starr] spent weeks, hundreds and hundreds of man-hours, trying to find out if [a deal existed between Clinton and Merletti], because when he asked me, I said, 'Wait a minute, I can tell you right now that never happened.'"

One facet of the claim of a secret deal that Bittman and others at OIC believed concerned a conversation Merletti had with Clinton when he was the agent in charge of the president's detail.

"Who could possibly be behind this story of you having a private conversation with the president?" I asked.

Merletti described it to me as if it had happened yesterday.

"I *did* have a conversation with Clinton. I got a call from the director, and he told me, 'We've got this newspaper story that's come out and we've discussed it back at headquarters, and we think you need to go see the president about this onboard Air Force One.'"

On Thursday, October 31, 1996, a letter appeared in the opinion section of the *Orange County Register* entitled "A Secret Service Agent Who Guarded Clinton Speaks Up."

Five days before the presidential election, retired agent Ron Williams offered his opinion of Bill Clinton.

"The reason I retired," Williams wrote, "was because I had become disenchanted with the egotistical arrogance of the Clinton staff and because I saw character flaws in Clinton."

Aboard Air Force One, on their way to Los Angeles for a campaign appearance, Merletti was tasked with telling the president what was about to become very public on the eve of the '96 election.

"You can't hide this thing," Merletti told me. "So, as hard as it was, I went in and talked to him."

Clinton wanted to know if the agent had ever served on his protective detail.

"No," he told the president.

He was surprised that a former agent would submit such a story to a newspaper.

"Sir," Merletti said, "we're as taken aback as you."

"I mean, *that's* what happened in terms of a personal conversation with the president," Merletti said. "Did I tell some people that story? Yes. Did they take it and twist it out of context? Somebody sure did. It's the old thing where you line up ten people and begin with the first, whispering a story, and by the time it gets to the end of the line, it's distorted."

One day before the election, the *Register* printed a response to the Williams letter from Secret Service Director Bowron:

> I am compelled to write in the strongest possible terms that we are incensed at the unprofessional and totally inappropriate behavior by Williams. He has done a disservice to the organization he once served. Ron Williams was assigned to our Los Angeles field office, had little or no contact with President Clinton, and in fact, retired 30 days after the president was inaugurated. His opinions are his as an individual and should not be given credibility . . . They are totally disavowed by the Secret Service.
>
> —Eljay B. Bowron, Washington, DC.

Four days after Bowron's response appeared in the paper, Williams sent a letter to the director.

"I want to apologize to the men and women of the US Secret Service for the article I wrote to the *Orange County Register*," Williams said. "I am sorry for the embarrassment and ramifications my letter caused."

The other facet of the secret deal claim came from a December 8, 1997, letter obtained by OIC, written by the president of the Association of Former Agents of the US Secret Service. The letter was among many documents Merletti shared with me from his files as director during our first interview. I also located a copy in OIC files.

The association letter cites a December 5, 1997, memo from Director Merletti to "All Employees" about the November publication of *The Dark Side of Camelot*. The book, authored by Seymour Hersh and released in the fall of 1997, was an exposé of former president John F. Kennedy, had quickly climbed the bestsellers list.

Hersh, an investigative reporter, gained prominence for exposing the My Lai massacre and cover-up during the Vietnam War. His book on Kennedy offered several first-person accounts from former agents on the president's detail about his many sexual indiscretions.

"He interviewed these four Secret Service guys," Merletti described, "and the fact that they would come out and talk about Kennedy's private life, I was stunned."

While Kennedy's agents were aware of the president's sexual comings and goings, they never took part in procuring women. That job was usually performed by David Powers, JFK's longtime personal aide. Nonetheless, one agent Hersh interviewed gave long and detailed accounts of the president's habits. Others spoke of the effects on the president's wife, Jackie.

Some of Kennedy's former agents contacted the director. "We came forward about Kennedy," they said. "You need to tell what you know about Clinton."

What angered Merletti was that agents were sharing personal information about a US president, a clear violation of the service's trust and confidence tenet.

After the book's release, "I sent out a nationwide teletype by the agency saying, 'This is unacceptable,'" Merletti told me.

He then contacted the head of the former agents' association to put out a press release to all members echoing the director's statement.

The December 1997 memo states, in part:

Four former Secret Service agents are quoted in the book as contributing information regarding the behavior of [President Kennedy]. This disclosure, regardless of its accuracy, is very troubling and counterproductive to the mission of the Secret Service. . . .

I ask that we all remember our commission book oath as "being worthy of trust and confidence." This is a confidence that should continue forever.

"Within a month, maybe six weeks," Merletti said, "the Monica Lewinsky thing happened, and Starr says, 'You knew we were coming. So you used this opportunity to blast people and tell them not to talk.' And I said, 'It didn't happen that way. Six weeks ago, I did not know that you were going to call us to testify.'"

When I mentioned the date of Merletti's memo coming before anyone had even heard the name Monica Lewinsky, former deputy Sol Wisenberg said, "That might have been before Lewinsky, but we were into the fourth or fifth year of our investigation, and you had the Paula

Jones thing going hot and heavy. So the fact that it was before Lewinsky is not impressive to me."

Wisenberg believed that the Secret Service director "had a special relationship with President Clinton" and that the director's battle against having agents testify was obstruction.

"I was appalled by Merletti's efforts to block [agents' testimony]," Wisenberg said, "and his efforts, as you know, were completely rejected in the courts. I think it was totally fucking hypocritical because there had been many Secret Service agents that have been allowed to write books, and nobody said anything about it. Now, suddenly, it was an issue. So I thought it was a fucking joke."

In fact, Merletti showed me two other memos related to confidentiality written by two previous directors. One of many documents he shared from his files was a March 26, 1996, memo entitled "Safeguarding Communications."

Then-director Eljay Bowron wrote, "Breaches of confidentiality and security undermine the confidence of protectees in our ability to carry out our mandate. Inadvertent or deliberate breaches will not be tolerated."

In another memo dated August 20, 1993, then-director John Magaw cited three articles by *Newsweek* magazine, "which contained inaccurate, unsubstantiated rumors about the service. Both the staff and I are concerned about the stories' detrimental effect not only on our mission but on the morale of our employees."

In his letter to *Newsweek* president and editor-in-chief Richard Smith, Magaw wrote:

Our agency has protected this nation's leaders for 92 years— and done so with devotion to duty, honor, courage, and integrity. This is the 17th time the Secret Service has assisted in the transition of a new President. Throughout each of these transitions, the Service has remained cognizant of the trust and confidence that must be maintained in its relationship with every individual it protects. This principle is as deeply ingrained in the Secret Service as the commitment to successfully and professionally accomplish our protective mandate.

"I was not the first one to be saying we shouldn't be talking about this," Merletti said. "So, when it hits with me, and I take the position that everyone has taken, now suddenly *I'm* the scoundrel. I'm not there standing on principle. We're covering up!"

"Starr's position," I suggested, "was that agents were covering up as far back as Kennedy, so why wouldn't they be covering up now?"

"Yes," Merletti said. "Here's what our point was: if we see a crime, we're going to report it. What they wanted—they wanted us to talk about the everyday life of the president of the United States.

"Now if you're the president of the United States, or better yet, *I'm* the president of the United States, and you're my chief counsel, and we just came into the White House after I'm out talking about stuff in front of the Secret Service guys, are you going to pull the president aside and say, 'Hey, everything you say, they're going to be out there telling everybody.'

"It's so logical," Merletti said. "If we see a crime, we'll report it. Anything else lights up, forget it. We're not talking about it."

Merletti was going through more papers. "I want to get to this."

"What are these?" I asked as he handed me some photocopies.

"Old, old documents," he described as he began reading from a "Memorandum for Secretary Norton; Protection of the President; June 8, 1910":

The danger is not imaginary—history has proven that. Admitting then, that there is danger, how can the President best be protected?

In this connection, I wish to say that the men of this service detailed at the Presidential home in Washington or elsewhere are instructed not to talk of anything they may see or hear. So far as the actions of the President and his family and social or official callers are concerned the men [agents] are deaf, dumb and blind. In all the years this service has been maintained at the White House and the freedom with which many important public matters have been discussed in the presence, there never has been a leak or betrayal of trust.

"This was written by the director," Merletti explained, "who was then called chief back in 1910. I have teletypes, messages. This is what we stand on. It's not just my idea. It's *everyone's* idea. This is what we need to be able to be there to protect the president of the United States.

"Let me make sure I've made this clear," Merletti emphasized. "I told them *repeatedly*, every time I gave a presentation, the Secret Service is law enforcement. If we saw a crime, you wouldn't have to ask us—we'd report it! I would have been the agent in charge of the president's detail. I would have gone to my director. I would have gone to the secretary of the Treasury. I witnessed a crime; I'm reporting it. We hadn't witnessed a crime! And Starr said, 'I want your guys to tell me, did women ever go in there and when they came out, their lipstick wasn't on right? Did you ever hear any sounds, did you ever see women . . . ?' It was ridiculous, absolutely ridiculous. I said, 'You *are* kidding?'

"'No,' Starr said. 'That's what I want to know.'

"We're in two *totally* different worlds," Merletti emphasized. "We're not there thinking, 'Jane Doe went in there at 8:18'; we wouldn't even know!"

Eleven days before the Rehnquist decision, one section of an internal OIC memo entitled "Direct Observations of the President and Monica Lewinsky in a Compromising Position" contained a list of agents and potential information OIC should follow up. Most of the information concerned the "movie theater" and "northwest gate" incidents.

The movie theater episode described a rumor of a "walk-in" by an agent, or someone known by the agent, allegedly observing Clinton and Lewinsky in a "compromising position" in the White House movie theater.

Despite a statement in the memo which reads, "We recently received information that tends to indicate that it may have actually happened," I could not locate any document in OIC's files that corroborated the incident and Lewinsky never testified about the incident under oath.

The widely reported northwest gate incident described Lewinsky showing up unannounced at the White House gate with gifts intended for the president that she wanted to pass to Clinton secretary Betty Currie. When Lewinsky reportedly learned that Eleanor Mondale was in the Oval Office with Clinton, she became "Very upset. Hysterical," she told a grand jury.

In two pages of the memo, an OIC attorney breaks down alleged observations and/or communications by some fifteen uniformed agents. Among them, I found this notation adjacent to an agent's name:

[Agent] has the following PFP [protective function privilege] observations/communications: (1) an incident that we really don't know anything about; (2) a number of privileged communications connected with the 12/6/97 Northwest Gate incident; (3) a privileged observation from [security posts] that does not relate to Monica; and (4) a PFP observation by [first agent], which was related to [a second agent] by someone other than [the first agent].

Although not all the notations were this eccentric, all relied on speculation, hearsay, rumor, "mysterious conversations," and privileged conversations. Of the fifteen Secret Service agents from the Uniformed Division identified in the memo, all but four had information related to the northwest gate incident—an episode that had nothing to do with security issues or criminal activity, only Lewinsky's anger about a woman in the Oval Office with Clinton.

The other four discussed "a second source for something we already know," "a PFP rumor," and two that talked about "hearsay communications that are privileged."

On January 27, *The Dallas Morning News* reported that a current or former Secret Service agent claimed to have witnessed Clinton and Lewinsky in an "ambiguous incident." Hours later, the paper retracted the story when their primary source "had provided us incorrect information," the paper's editor stated. Before the correction was printed, however, the wire service had already spread the false information and a New York tabloid carried the headline: "Secret Service agent to testify: I SAW THEM DO IT."

Ultimately, the truth came out. The agent had only witnessed Lewinsky enter the Oval Office on several occasions but saw or heard nothing else.

"There are other doors in and out of the Oval Office," Merletti described. "You could go in one door and thirty seconds later go out another door, and [the first agent wouldn't] see it.

In fact, in her third interview at the independent counsel's office, Monica Lewinsky stated that she "purposely departed by a different door than the one she had entered, so that the USSS staff would not know when Lewinsky came and left."

"We came to learn," Merletti said, "that [this uniformed agent] made it his business to know about a number of women's personal lives . . . all very unprofessional. We had complaints from a number of men and women that worked in the West Wing regarding the comments he made regarding women. He was ID'd as the source of many rumors."

Starr "assigned scores of FBI agents," Merletti notated, "to investigate wild and salacious rumors about USSS conduct—which were all disproved—when the FBI agents should have been investigating terrorist cases that were developing right here in the US. This was the same time frame that the 9/11 hijackers were here in the US planning and training for their attacks."

Merletti handed me another document. "What's this?"

"This is Carl Rowan. He gets it!" Merletti was referencing an article from *The Buffalo News*, May 28, 1998, entitled, "Common Sense and the Secret Service."

"There is an uncodified, common-sense rule," Rowan wrote, "that ought to apply in the Lewinsky case where special prosecutor Kenneth Starr is trying to force Secret Service agents to testify. That rule is that no one can force the agents who guard the president and his family to become mere tattletales and gossips."

Merletti handed me more.

The Philadelphia Inquirer, May 2, 1998, "Starr Mistook His Job as Hunt for the Truth Instead of Justice."

The New York Times, May 30, 1998, "Shaped by a Painful Past, Secret Service Director Fights Required Testimony."

The Wall Street Journal, June 4, 1998, "Secret Service Privilege: A Matter of Life or Death."

In a June 16, 1998, *Washington Post* story, under the headline, "Assassination Risk Cited in Ex-Agents' Brief to Block Queries," journalist Peter Baker wrote, "those who filed a brief included three other agents involved in assassination attempts: Timothy J. McCarthy, who was shot by Hinckley while guarding Reagan; Larry Buendorf, who stopped Lynette 'Squeaky' Fromme from killing Gerald R. Ford in 1975; and Nick J. Zarvos, who was wounded when Arthur Bremer shot and crippled presidential candidate George C. Wallace in 1972."

The brief was in support of Director Merletti's argument.

"I was against having agents testify," McCarthy said. "If the president [Reagan] had said to me, 'Tim, I have to have a private conversation with Mike Deaver, would you just step forward a little so you won't hear?'—the round that hit me would have hit the president."

Chris Von Holt, another agent brought before Ken Starr's grand jury, publicly stated:

Our function is to protect the people elected to office. We're non-political. We don't have any interest in what the protectee is doing politically with Congress . . . We don't have any interest in what the protectee does in his or her personal life, and we should be there as people fulfilling our mission.

"Robert L. DeProspero, who headed Reagan's security detail for six years," Baker wrote, "recalled the example of a threatening letter-writer who called himself 'Catman.' When agents finally caught the man on a New York City subway, they discovered photographs showing that he had been just outside the fence at Gracie Mansion during an event, close enough to fire at the president, but with his shot seemingly blocked by agents."

Edward P. Walsh, who protected LBJ and Nixon, said, "If you don't have trust and confidence, you don't have proximity. If you don't have proximity, you have an open door. . . . Some bad guy is going to walk through that open door."

"That's nonsense," former Kennedy agent, Tony Sherman told investigative reporter Seymour Hersh. "Presidents ask agents to step aside any time they are too close when they play golf. The [security] system is difficult to overcome. I don't think a president will think, 'The guys are going to blab about whatever I say.'"

The *Post* story also cited four former attorneys general, William P. Barr, Griffin B. Bell, Edwin Meese III, and Richard L. Thornburgh, who believed that agents should testify.

Others sided with the Secret Service.

Theodore Sorensen, special counsel to President Kennedy, wrote, "Compelling testimony from those entrusted with the security of the President diminishes the very purpose of their existence. To invite this and every future president's mistrust and avoidance of those responsible for his or her safety is to invite tragedy."

Constitutional scholar and Harvard law professor Laurence Tribe
wrote:

> In essence, the courts have held that, if a privilege for the
> President's bodyguards is to be created, Congress will have
> to create it. Some say the privilege is unnecessary because no
> President would knowingly risk his life by holding those who
> guard him at arm's length. How naive! Presidents already hate
> having their freedom constricted by the constant presence of
> the Secret Service. . . . And a President cannot know which
> of his actions or conversations might in hindsight be deemed
> relevant to a criminal inquiry of some sort. With the exception
> for direct observation of a crime in progress, compelling
> agents to testify about what they saw or overheard represents
> a dubious trade.

"Look at this here," Merletti said, handing me a copy of *The
Washington Post* (February 6, 1998) and *USA Today* (February 5, 1998),
both of which carried diagrams of the West Wing. "This is *exactly* what
I didn't want. Someone from Al-Qaeda, 'Well, look at this, this is exactly
where all the offices are.'

"What [Starr] did was over the top," Merletti said. "He did not use
good judgment. He went way beyond the parameters of common sense.
He became like a man possessed."

After receiving the first subpoenas for agent testimony at Secret
Service headquarters, Merletti went to historian Mike Sampson.

"'Mike,' I said, 'I need you to research every time the Secret Service
was pushed away. And the result was the protectee was either hurt or
killed.'

"I had received probably dozens [of media requests] . . . Larry King, Tim Russert from *Meet the Press*, but the Secret Service felt, which means, I felt, that our job wasn't to be out there getting face time. Our job was to protect the president of the United States, to quietly go about our job and still get our message out, somehow.

"Our public relations department would schedule three, four, five of these people to come in at a time, and I'd spend three hours with them and would give them this presentation. I think I wore them out. But when they left, everyone one of them said, 'You are right. You're definitely right.'

"And they would say, 'Can you get this down to a half hour, and come on our TV show?' 'I don't want to do that,' I said. 'I want this to be resolved in a professional manner. I don't want to take it to the American public unless I must.'"

Merletti took me through more of his presentation to Starr.

"In 1901, we're protecting [President] McKinley, and he attends the Buffalo Exposition, and he's standing there, and an official at the exposition wanted to be on his right side where an agent was standing. So, he said to the president, 'Can you ask Agent McIntyre to step aside, sir? Nobody's gonna hurt you.'

"Now this is 1901, and we're not officially assigned protection, but we're with him. These are the things we recognize. So McIntyre steps aside. Within moments, Leon Czolgosz puts a gun to his stomach, shoots McKinley, who dies several days later. There's a perfect example of an agent who's been pushed away.

"At one point, Ken Starr asked, 'Why isn't President Clinton telling you what to do? Tell him that you guys are going to talk.'

"I said, 'It's not his decision to ever tell me to do anything. It's not his job. I don't answer to him. I have the greatest respect for the office of the presidency, but I know what my mission is. And that's how I became the agent in charge on a presidential detail because I understood my mission. I was there to make sure the Secret Service mission was not compromised.

"The person who's in charge of the detail has a relationship with the president," Merletti described. "If the president asks me, 'I want to do something different,' I have to explain to him why, and I have to be firm. Not bullheaded, firm.

"I gave the McKinley example in my presentation to Starr twice; to the Justice Department once; to Janet Reno once, and they picked parts out and gave it in court. Now, I was allowed to be in both courtrooms, but when the case went before the Supreme Court, I wasn't even allowed to be there."

"What was the reaction from friends and family to all of this?" I asked.

"I'd say it was mixed. It was mixed along political lines. It seemed to me, rather than the truth, people wanted a soap opera. I think a lot of people were led to believe that we were involved in a big cover-up. Once I explained a few things, they said, 'Yeah, we shouldn't have agents testify.'

"I've been in the Secret Service for twenty-five years," Merletti said. "I started working in West Philadelphia on Treasury check cases. I've interviewed people that were struggling in life, had no education, no food, nothing. When I was based in New York, I worked in the Bronx, Brooklyn; I worked in ghettos, you name it. I understand people. I had never seen *anyone* like Starr. I couldn't get him to see common sense. It was like he didn't understand the language I was speaking.

"It was all about politics. It had nothing to do with the truth," Merletti said, shaking his head. "That's why I'm so disappointed in Ken Starr. So many people said he was such a good man. Something was driving him, because I laid out *exactly* what the truth was. I laid out what the threats were, what the threat to our nation was, and he couldn't care less."

"Rather than the truth, people wanted a soap opera . . . all about politics" – virtually the identical wording Merletti used to describe his experience sitting before the House subcommittee questioning him about the Treasury report on the Waco matter.

History was repeating itself. Only this time, Merletti was being accused of aiding and covering up an improper relationship between the president and a White House intern by the independent counsel for personal gain. Nevertheless, Starr and his deputies had an additional piece of information that solidified their belief in a secret deal between Merletti and the president—a letter addressed to Ken Starr, signed "Deep Throat."

14

At 8:00 a.m. on Thursday, July 16, 2015, I received an email from Robert Reed, my contact at the archives. It concerned a list of documents I had requested from the Office of Independent Counsel files regarding the Secret Service matter.

"Jim . . . Folder 23 also has a June 6, 1998 letter (signed Deep Throat) . . . I don't think I'll be able to check these files until next week."

In the many conversations I'd had with Merletti, he frequently said, "[Starr] had some 'Deep Throat' type of information, and he believed this information, and it could not have been further from the truth."

While Bob Woodward's Deep Throat had been a true source, Starr's source was built upon a collection of half-truths, rumors, assumptions, and other information: Clinton's alleged "finger in the chest" to Merletti in the White House; Merletti's private conversation with Clinton onboard Air Force One informing him of a former agent's letter in an LA newspaper; the ensuing talk that circulated around the Secret Service; the release of the Hersh book, *The Dark Side of Camelot*, where agents disclosed information about President Kennedy's personal life; and the directive Merletti sent out to agents as well as the association of former agents reminding them to remain silent about the personal business and conversations of protectees, a critical piece of the Secret Service *trust and confidence* tenet. Now comes a letter from a source *inside* the Secret Service.

All of this fed the false narrative that Merletti had cut a deal with Clinton to remain silent regarding what he knew about Clinton's relationship with Lewinsky in exchange for becoming director of the Secret Service.

I nearly fell out of my chair when I received the email, and responded to Reed within minutes: "Rob, really critical: Would it be possible for you to send me copies of the last two items on your list before next week?"

The following day, Reed sent me scanned copies of three faxed documents from the independent counsel. The header on the fax indicates that the first two pages were sent to the Washington office on January 29, 1998.

The first page is a copy of a letter from the Association of Former Agents of the Secret Service that talks about Director Merletti's reaction to the Hersh book and his statement that former agents should never discuss details of a protectee's private life. A copy of the letter was among several documents Merletti gave me from his files as director at our first meeting.

The second page appears to have been drafted by someone other than the Secret Service insider (Merletti's name is misspelled). It could be the third party that Bittman spoke of who passed along information from the source. "Merletti told someone at the Secret Service [of his deal with Clinton], and that person whom he told, 'Joe Smith,' told someone else who was *not* in the Secret Service, and *that* someone told us."

The second page explains how to find people within the Secret Service and others who come and go from the White House. Whoever prepared it had access to information from someone with knowledge of Secret Service protocols.

The third page appears to have come directly from the source inside the Service and was faxed five months later.

June 06, 1998

The Honorable Kenneth W. Starr

Independent Counsel

Office of the Independent Counsel

1001 Pennsylvania Ave., N.W.

Suite 490-North

Washington, DC

Dear Judge Starr,

If you would like an official record of the whereabouts of POTUS, as far back as 1991, you should subpoena the shift reports of the US Secret Service. The records will be kept by the Office of Protective Operations, Presidential Protective Division. These records are prepared by individual Shift Leaders, for each 8-hour shift, three each day. These records not only show where POTUS was on a particular day and how he traveled there, the report also discloses who met with him. Each time permanent staff come and go are not generally recorded, but I'd bet that there are records of Monica Lewinsky's meeting with POTUS, especially after she left the White House.

The above referred to records are prepared by Secret Service Agents, not Uniformed Officers. UD does keep records of people entering and leaving the White House grounds outer perimeter. The Shift report will be a much more informative report, are kept at least ten years (probably more), and are easily and quickly retrieved. Why not make your subpoena *duces tecum*, produce the records right now?

Also, be advised there is a rumor among USSS personnel that both Director Merletti and the current PPD SAIC have compromised themselves and their positions by having had illicit sexual affairs with female WH Staff members. They are both married men. If this is true, it is time they retired. — Sincerely, Deep Throat

The header on the fax on the first two pages has the date when it was sent, the sender's phone number, the name of the sender, and a page number.

The phone number from the sender had a 501-area code, the area code of Little Rock, Arkansas. According to OIC records, the number matched one of two fax lines at the Centerville Drive address in Little Rock where deputy Hickman Ewing worked. The name of the sender: "INDEP COUNSEL."

Prior to his tenure as deputy independent counsel in the Little Rock office, W. Hickman Ewing Jr., had been the US attorney for the Western District of Tennessee for ten years where he developed a taste for prosecuting political corruption. Ewing's task in Little Rock centered around Hillary Clinton's work at the Rose Hill Law Center and oversight of the Clintons' involvement in the Whitewater Development Corporation.

The Deep Throat letter was likely sent to DC sometime around June 6, 1998, the date on the letter. However, at the top of the letter, near the upper-right-hand corner, was a handwritten initial, "E." Below the body of the letter were handwritten notes: "Fax to: KS, SW, PR, RH, JB, BB."

All three pages were together in one folder in Robert Bittman's work files. All three pages appeared to have been sent from Little Rock to the Washington office with instructions to fax to everyone on the list, presumably to their homes. None of the documents were noted in OIC's timeline of the Secret Service matter, nor were they mentioned in Starr's handwritten notes.

The initial "E" at the top of the letter appeared to identify Hickman Ewing. I discovered a second document in Bittman's work files that carried the handwritten initials, "H.E.," in the upper right-hand corner of that document. The cursive letter "E" appears identical to that on the Deep Throat letter.

This would suggest that Starr's secret source delivered the pages to Ewing. When Ewing faxed the pages to the Washington office, he gave instructions at the bottom of the page to fax copies to Ken Starr, Solomon Wisenberg, Paul Rosenzweig, Rodger Heaton, Jackie Bennett, and Bob Bittman. I checked the initials against the DC staff directory. The names were later confirmed by Rosenzweig.

Although many of the former prosecutors I interviewed had hazy memories, I thought I had a better chance with Ewing, considering what Ken Starr wrote about him in his 2019 memoir, *Contempt*, about the Clinton investigation.

Starr writes that he "would have been unable to recount many of the details without the invaluable insight—and astonishing recall—of

Hickman Ewing. His daily journal was an unerring source of lively details."

It sounded like Ewing's memory and journal were just the sources that would help answer a lot of questions. I sent a letter and left four voice messages on Ewing's phone requesting an interview.

No response.

I sent the documents to Merletti. His reaction to the Deep Throat letter was immediate: "I feel like I've been victimized all over again."

While Ken Starr declined multiple interview requests and Jackie Bennett did not respond, I reached out to others on the list.

In an email, I asked former associate independent counsel Rodger Heaton, "Can you recall any details from looking at the Deep Throat letter?"

Heaton's response: "Unfortunately, no. But if you haven't talked to Paul Rosenzweig, you should try. He is likely to have a better memory than I do."

Senior litigation counsel Paul Rosenzweig's email response: "I am sorry, but I really don't have a direct memory of this. My vague recollection is that we did go get the shift records, at some point, in addition to the UD [uniformed Division] records, but I'm not even sure of that. . . . I do agree that the PR is almost certainly me, as it was that the BB is Bittman and that SW is Sol Wisenberg, etc."

Responding to additional questions, Rosenzweig writes: "I never met the tipster. I don't even know if he exists, nor do I have any reason to think he was telling the truth (or telling a falsity), nor do I recall us ever corroborating the rumor of sexual misconduct. Nor do I know what Director Merletti's reaction to this was. Sorry, I think I was a courtesy copy on this. You really have exhausted my knowledge. I think

Wisenberg and Bittman were much more engaged and would defer to them."

"Courtesy" copied? . . . on a document listing only six OIC attorneys containing possible whistleblower evidence that the director of the Secret Service was colluding with the president to obstruct a federal investigation?

After my interview with Bittman abruptly ended, I immediately sent a letter apologizing for any misunderstanding regarding his response to the court questions. I included the original set of questions I had in front of me at the time of our interview, willing to accept any written responses he may wish to offer.

No response. That door appeared closed.

In our first interview, I asked Wisenberg about the Secret Service tip. Although this seemed to be an important lead to Starr, Bittman, and Bennett, Wisenberg didn't remember much, even sounding nonchalant.

"What can you tell me about the Secret Service tip?" I asked.

"I really can't. I knew we got tips at various times. Doesn't surprise me."

"According to Bittman, everyone in the office knew about the tip, and you were one of the deputies in the office. Did you find any corroboration on this individual's story?"

"What I remember, there was some kind of feeling . . . ground rules on interviewing [the source]."

"Whatever you can tell me that can enlighten me about this story, Sol. I'm just interested in the truth."

"Gotta remember, it's been quite a while ago. I don't know about that deal. I don't know what corroborative efforts were made. That wasn't something that was part of what I was doing."

After sending him a copy of the Deep Throat letter, Wisenberg began by saying that he didn't have a fax machine in his office. (I neglected to ask if he had one at home, which would have made sense for everyone on the list.) After reading the letter, he repeated, three times, during our conversation, "Why is this so important? We got lots of tips. What makes this so special?"

"I would think that a tip that comes from inside the Secret Service would receive priority attention."

He just repeated his stance, and the conversation ended.

Even though Wisenberg characterized the Lewinsky matter as "the case of the century"—a case in which the Secret Service was inextricably entwined—he could not recall the details of a tip and letter from inside the Secret Service.

I asked Robert Reed at the archives to send me all tips in OIC files. Only nine emails were found, along with some handwritten letters. However, as Bittman pointed out, "some are crazy." I assume many came into the office by phone and were just too "crazy" to record.

Of the nine emails Reed sent, all are in a much older format than current emails. One is signed "Deepthroat"; a second lists the email's "creator" as "deepthroat." However, none has a date that fits the time frame of the Secret Service matter. None mentions the Secret Service, and none offers the specific information that the Deep Throat letter to Ken Starr offers.

I tried looking for copies of the letter in the work files of all prosecutors listed at the bottom of the letter, thinking that perhaps other copies had notes. I found none.

I find this surprising, considering that the Federal Records Act of 1950 directs that "The head of each Federal agency shall make and preserve records . . . [including those] received by an agency of the United States Government."

But if copies of the Deep Throat letter sent to others had notes, like the Ewing copy, wouldn't they constitute new documents?

I asked Reed about this.

In his experience, Reed writes, "Copies of the same document filed in multiple attorney files are not considered duplicates because each attorney would be expected to retain his or her own copy. Annotated copies containing additional information are treated as distinct from a true duplicate that is not annotated. That being said, many individuals who create and maintain files subject to the Federal Records Act do not always fulfill their obligations under the act."

Reed added, "It's always possible that other copies of the letter exist within the Starr records—the collection comprises well over three thousand boxes of files. However, using the file manifests created by OIC, which are the only available finding aids, I was unable to locate another copy in any of the files searched. It's hard to say definitively that no other copies were retained by OIC attorneys, but if other annotated copies were similarly identified in the file manifests, I believe they would have been located."

If Hickman Ewing maintained a daily journal of his activities as deputy independent counsel, as Starr describes, that journal may be part of a federal record and should have been retained in OIC's Little Rock files before being transferred to the archives. I could not locate any listing for Ewing's journal in either the Little Rock or DC manifests.

Again, I turned to Robert Reed.

"I'm not certain that Ewing's journal is a federal record. It could be considered a personal account of his service as Deputy Independent

Counsel, rather than his attorney work product created in his official capacity representing the OIC."

Possibly. But Ewing's journal might identify the Deep Throat source and hold additional information related to the Secret Service matter. Absent his journal in the archives, we'll never know.

Nonetheless, Starr and his deputies believed they had a perfect storm of tips and information: Linda Tripp's call to Jackie Bennett on January 12, 1998, informing OIC of the Clinton/Lewinsky relationship, which was true; Bennett's contact with a source inside the Secret Service tipping him that the Secret Service director helped facilitate the relationship—real contact, false tip; two documents faxed to the DC office from Little Rock on January 29 (before Merletti's presentation to Starr and Bittman), presumed to be evidence of collusion between the president and Merletti—real documents, false assumption; and that Lewis Merletti had been appointed Secret Service director during Clinton's second term as a result of his alleged deal with Clinton—a false assumption.

Now, five months later, comes a letter addressed directly to Ken Starr from their source offering additional information about learning the movements of the president and Monica Lewinsky.

Even though OIC had no corroboration of the Deep Throat tip, the convergence of all this information convinced Starr and his deputies, more than ever, that Merletti was deeply involved in a cover-up.

However, what the Deep Throat letter *did* confirm was that someone within the Service was waging a personal vendetta against the director.

15

With Starr's legal victory over the Secret Service's confidentiality privilege with the July 17 Rehnquist decision, Starr and his team began calling agents before a grand jury to inquire about the comings and goings of Monica Lewinsky.

On the evening of August 17, 1998, Clinton finally addressed the American people with the truth.

"Good evening. This afternoon in this room, from this chair, I testified before the Office of Independent Counsel and the grand jury. . . . Indeed, I *did* have a relationship with Miss Lewinsky that was not appropriate."

The following day, Kelleher arrived at Merletti's office.

"It's over, Lew."

Starr's investigators could find no evidence substantiating any special relationship between Clinton and Merletti and Secret Service agents beyond their official duties.

"Over?" Merletti reacted, anger building all over again. "They put us through seven months of total, senseless distraction only to have Starr admit what we all knew from the beginning?"

At that moment, a staffer entered, announcing that the independent counsel was on the phone.

"Director, Ken Starr. Well, it's over. The Secret Service was a dry hole. You knew nothing. I hope this is the only time in history that the Secret Service has to go through something like this."

Merletti was clenching his jaw throughout Starr's recital. "You didn't understand. You can't pull us into a political battle. Our fight was not about Clinton; it was about principle. It was about the Secret Service's ability to protect the office of the presidency."

Reflecting on the experience years later, Merletti remained indignant. "In all my years of experience, I had never met anyone with such an attitude of superiority. It was *all* about politics. It had nothing to do with the truth because I laid out exactly what the truth was, what the threats were, what the threat to our nation was, and he couldn't care less."

In a February 1998 interview for PBS, Ken Starr declared, "We are going by the book. We want the truth. We want all the truth. We want it completely, accurately, and we will satisfy ourselves that we're getting the truth. And that is the absolute bedrock point. We want the truth."

Former special counsel Jo Ann Harris observed, "Well, I really think Starr was over his head. I mean, he can talk about the truth all he wants, but he is, from what I can see, a very self-righteous person who really has no clue as to how to exercise judgment in very complicated situations. He is an academic, brilliant law guy," she reiterated, "and the worst possible kind of person you should put in charge of an independent counsel's office, and he's not the first."

On November 10, 1998, the front page of *The Washington Post* carried the following headline: "Judiciary Panel Signals It Will Pursue Impeachment."

Three days later, a much smaller story appeared in *The New York Times*: "Secret Service Director Retiring to Work for Pro Football Team."

At just twenty-one months, Merletti served one of the shortest terms as director in the history of the Secret Service, contradicting OIC's belief that he coveted the position.

You would think that the story ends here. It doesn't.

16

In January 2001, Merletti was in his Ohio office when he received a call from his Washington attorney, Warren Dennis.

"I just got a call from the FBI," Dennis told him. "They want to question you."

"About what?" Merletti asked.

"The whole Clinton thing."

"You mean this thing's *still* going on?"

"They're issuing you an invitation to talk."

"I decline the invitation."

"Lew, I spent my whole career getting my clients invited and not subpoenaed because if you go in there and say something that's not true, you'll go to jail."

"I'm not going," Merletti said.

"Lew, you don't understand. They will subpoena you within hours."

"Warren, *you* don't understand. They hurt my people. They hurt the Secret Service, and they think I'm going to come back . . . by invitation?"

On January 18, 2001, Merletti arrived in Washington expecting to face a grand jury. Instead, he walked into a large conference room at the office of his attorney. He was sitting for a pre–grand jury meeting. Among those in attendance was FBI Special Agent Jennifer Gant.

Merletti described the meeting as "a two-and-a-half-hour interrogation led by Gant. This was a contentious battle from the moment the door closed and I sat down. I had no time to say, 'Let me talk to you about protection and why I believe it's important.' There was *none* of that. I was on one side of a large conference table, and the opposition was on the other side."

Gant glared at Merletti. "You're the last person who can give us the information we need to criminally charge Bill Clinton before he leaves office in two days, and before we leave this meeting today, you *will* give us that information."

Merletti was stunned by what the agent said next.

"We have information that *you*, Mr. Merletti, went to the White House after hours; that you drove your car up the South Lawn, entered through the diplomatic reception area, brought the president out, put him in the back seat of your car, placed a blanket over him, and took him to a hotel where he met with Monica Lewinsky."

It was the identical narrative that Starr and Bittman told Merletti at his first meeting in the independent counsel's office, and all of it was based on false information provided by their Deep Throat source inside the Secret Service; all of it from a source who refused to go on the record; all of it without a shred of corroboration; and all of it contradicting what Ken Starr told Merletti after Secret Service agents testified, "You guys knew nothing whatsoever."

Moreover, Lewinsky was extensively interviewed by Starr's attorneys and had only mentioned Merletti once. In her third interview, an FBI agent noted, *Lewinsky saw a USSS plainclothes agent named Lou Merletti several times, but had more of an acquaintance than a friendship with him . . ."*

In all 18 interviews, 2 grand jury appearances, and a deposition, none of Starr's attorneys ever asked Lewinsky about Merletti's involvement in her relationship with Clinton. Nor did Lewinsky volunteer any such information.

Why should this matter?

Because the immunity deal Lewinsky signed with the independent counsel *required* that she "not attempt to protect any person or entity through false information or *omission*, and [that] she will not attempt falsely, to implicate any person or entity."

And no such line of questioning about Merletti's involvement took place during President Clinton's grand jury testimony. No questions from Robert Bittman, Solomon Wisenberg, Jackie Bennett and no questions from Ken Starr, all of whom believed that the president had a deal with the Secret Service director at the time.

"OK, hold it," Merletti told Gant. He wasn't going to sit through this fiction again. "Let's just stop for a second and logically think about this. You're alleging that I go to the White House in the evening. There is always a sizable number of security personnel on duty. Their job is to protect the president, and they go with him wherever he goes. Those are standing orders. There are no orders that I can give that would countermand those orders.

"So, according to your premise, I go upstairs, I get the president of the United States, and we walk past a number of agents that are posted.

I walk out the diplomatic reception room, put him in my car, and throw a blanket over him."

Merletti paused for emphasis. "And no one sees this?"

"OK," he continued, "let's move forward. I get in the car; I drive out the gate. That's all recorded in the movement logs: Merletti was here, he entered the White House, he left the White House.

"Now, we get to the hotel. So, where do I park? Do I park on the street, and the president and I walk into the hotel together, or do I park in the parking garage, and the president and I go up an elevator, go into the lobby, and I do all of this and *no one* sees me?

"Did I have the blanket over his head the whole time, and no one notices that I'm walking through a hotel lobby with this man with a blanket over his head? Do you see how absurd this is?" Merletti told Gant. "It can't happen; it didn't happen. It just doesn't make sense."

Nonetheless, the agent continued her interrogation, asking Merletti for all his calendars as director and details of how many times he saw the president during Lewinsky's time at the White House.

I contacted former associate independent counsel Monte Richardson who attended the meeting. In a phone conversation, I asked Richardson, now a magistrate judge, if he recalled the Merletti meeting in his work in Ray's office.

"I'm not in a position to comment," Richardson said. "I signed a confidentiality agreement, I believe, when I worked there, and I can't comment on anything that happened during my time with the independent counsel's office."

Surprised, I asked, "You signed a confidentiality agreement? Because I've spoken with several former OIC attorneys, and the subject of such an agreement never came up."

"I sure remember signing one," Richardson said without hesitation.

"So, you can't discuss any aspect of that meeting?"

"I really don't recall any details about it. In any event, I can't comment on it as well," Richardson added.

"Well, I don't want you to violate your agreement, Judge."

I asked Robert Reed at the archives if he had ever come across any confidentiality agreements signed by OIC attorneys.

"I don't recall seeing any confidentiality agreements," Reed said.

At this point, Reed had been searching the independent counsel files regarding the Secret Service matter on my behalf for five years and had become well acquainted with them. In his opinion, Reed said that he didn't believe Richardson would still be bound by such an agreement after the report was published. And I found no such agreement in Richardson's work files.

I called Richardson's office again. The judge was out. I gave his assistant my name and number.

"By the way," I added, "you might tell the judge that I've checked with the archives, and he may have his position at OIC confused with another federal post he held, because according to the archivist, he could not recall finding any confidentiality agreements in OIC files."

Richardson did not return my call.

In reviewing the endnotes in Ken Gormley's book, *The Death of American Virtue,* I came across an interesting passage regarding the Merletti meeting: "notes of the session, maintained by a source who wished to remain anonymous, confirmed that the initial questions were designed to determine if Merletti was 'colluding' with the president in carrying out his affair with Monica Lewinsky."

During my research, I was told that notes taken during that January meeting were to be destroyed. After sharing this and additional information, I persuaded a source with knowledge of the meeting to offer some details.

"The reason for the meeting," the source said, "was to determine if the [protective function] privilege was a sincerely held view or was an orchestrated effort to prevent evidence from coming forward to the independent counsel."

"Were notes kept of that meeting?" I asked.

"If there were notes, they would be in the archives. I mean well, I don't think that I had any notes on that."

"I'm asking because I haven't been able to locate any notes of that meeting in the archives."

"The volume of information that the National Archives collected from OIC, it would be like a needle in a haystack. So the answer to your question, do I have any notes? No, I don't believe I have any notes," he said. "If I had notes on that stuff, it would be because they were misplaced . . . but I don't think I have any notes on that."

I never asked the source if *he* had any notes, only if notes were kept.

"According to Merletti, Special Agent Gant asked a series of questions about his alleged collusion with President Clinton in which Merletti arranged trysts between the president and Monica Lewinsky in exchange for being appointed director. Do you recall any of the questions Gant asked Merletti?"

"Jennifer Gant was a very skilled FBI agent, and she may have asked questions that she perceived to be important that I wouldn't have even been consulted or know anything about. Also present was Bob Ray. So the questions were really asked by Robert Ray and her."

"Robert Ray was not there," Merletti told me, confirming this with a copy of business cards from everyone in attendance.

"I think somebody called me a couple of years ago," the source described. "I think someone wrote a book on this."

"Ken Gormley."

"Yeah, Ken Gormley asked me some questions about this, and then I had something that he asked me about and, fortuitously, as I was going through some stuff, I found it, and I don't remember what it was. I think I sent it to him . . . The reason why I'm so vague is because although [Merletti] was my witness, I don't believe he was ever called before the grand jury for us."

"You mentioned that you found something that you sent to Ken."

As I'm taking notes, there is a clear silence on the other end of the line.

"Honestly, I'm not lying to you. You can find out from him if I gave him notes. I don't remember what I found because I don't believe we kept stuff.

"What I remember is this. I remember that I talked to [Gormley], and then I was going through something, and there was a piece of paper that I had that was not even in the right file, and I just happened to come across it, and I was very surprised by it. So, I called him back because I felt like I almost misrepresented things when I said I don't have anything. I sent that to him."

More silence.

"Honestly, I'm not trying to be any more avoiding with you than I was with him when I found it. I just don't recall what it was, but if he was talking to me about Merletti, it may have had something to do with that."

"Did you send that document to Ken?"

"I sent something to him. I don't know if it was *that* document."

"If I speak to Ken about our conversation and mention the document, would you mind my asking?"

"I don't mind you asking him. If he feels uncomfortable, he should call and tell me. I don't know exactly what we're talking about. I vaguely remember that I may have sent it to him."

During our interview, I wrote, "He's halting . . . cautious . . . uncomfortable." More silence before I read the passage about the notes from Gormley's book.

"I'm just looking to get the facts as clearly as possible. I'm not out to—"

"No, no, I'm not playing a game here."

"I know you're not."

"What I'm trying to say is that I don't want to say I did something and then have to walk that back when I find out I didn't do it. I heard what you read, and I don't know if that's what I had. It may have been. I don't remember."

"I'm just trying to obtain the most accurate account of what took place in that meeting, and I hope you'll understand this in the right light when I ask this question: Are *you* the anonymous source that talks about these notes?"

He laughed. "I don't know. I've never *even* read the book, and I don't even know what the notes are. I don't know if I'm an anonymous source or not."

"OK, fair enough."

"That's what I'm saying. I never saw his book, although I intended to get it. And I don't even know now what the notes are if there were notes. As you can see, my recollection was completely wrong, because I didn't even remember that Monte was there. I thought it was Bob Ray."

After offering to send him a copy of Gormley's book, he agreed to a follow-up.

I tried multiple times to reconnect and only reached an answering machine. In a letter, I reminded him of our conversation and his agreement for a follow-up.

In response, he wrote, "I don't remember the questions that were asked, but I do remember Special Agent Gant asking pointed questions."

That confirmed Merletti's account.

"My present recollection is that after the interview, I was convinced Mr. Merletti's intentions were genuine.

"As to the allegation that I was instructed to destroy any notes, I deny that happened, at least in the context you suggest. When we left OIC we were instructed to leave all OIC material. I recall making every effort to comply with this requirement. I was never instructed to destroy my personal notes of Mr. Merletti's interview. I doubt I even had such notes."

I was puzzled by his statement denying that he "was never instructed to destroy any notes, *at least in the context you suggest.*"

He appeared to imply that he destroyed something. But what other context was he talking about? The Federal Records Act *requires* the preservation of documents related to federal activities.

"As I told you in our telephone conversation, after speaking with Mr. Gormley, I discovered a piece of paper in an old file, unrelated to my time at OIC, that was relevant to my conversation with Mr. Gormley. I called him and told him about it. I may have sent him a copy, but I don't have a certain recollection that I did. I have searched for this document again but haven't found it. As I recall, it was a list of topics to be covered, sort of an agenda. They were pre-interview, not post-interview, notes. This I know: I do not have any personal notes taken during or after Mr. Merletti's interview."

The letter was cloudy and suggested contradictions. In our phone conversation, he said that Merletti was *his* witness. In the letter, he says that Merletti was Richardson's witness. OK, that could be a reasonable memory lapse.

In my interview, he said, "I had something that [Gormley] asked me about and, fortuitously . . . I found it."

In the letter, he says the paper was "unrelated to my time at OIC." If the paper was unrelated, why would he then describe it as "a list of topics to be covered, sort of an agenda. They were pre-interview, not post-interview notes [regarding the Merletti meeting]"?

In his letter, he wrote, "I doubt I even had such notes. . . . I have searched for this document again but haven't found it."

In our interview, he said, "I just happened to come across it, and I was very surprised by it. I sent that to him [Gormley].

In the letter, he says, "I *may* have sent him a copy."

In our phone conversation, the source clearly seemed anxious when I mentioned these notes. During our conversation, he suddenly said, "I'm not lying."

In all my interviews, I never suggest anyone is lying. I'm always seeking the most accurate recollection of past events. However, despite his inconsistencies and apparent apprehension, I *never* found a "smoking gun" identifying him as Gormley's anonymous source. Nevertheless, our discussion about the notes of the Merletti meeting sure made him uncomfortable.

Near the end of my interview, I asked, "So, you never believed that Merletti's purpose was to cover up for the president?"

"No. I don't recall seeing anything that would support that allegation," he said.

I contacted Ken Gormley about the "paper," asking if he would share those notes. Ken was very generous with his time but was unable to locate the document in question. As to the issue of whether my source was Gormley's anonymous source, Gormley, an honorable man who wishes to protect his sources just as I protect mine, did not offer any additional information.

After that January 18, 2001, meeting, the source said, "We all walked away with the opinion that [Merletti] was a very credible person. And . . . if he wasn't called before the grand jury, it was because there was a decision made that, 'Hey, there was no collusion here. Why are we wasting our time?'"

17

I made four requests to interview Ken Starr; all were declined. However, I was able to access special counsels' interview of Starr, as well as more than three hundred pages of his handwritten notes from the archives. Along with his 2019 memoir, *Contempt*, about the Clinton investigation, they offer additional insight into Starr's handling of the Lewinsky and Secret Service matters.

In our interview, Harris repeatedly mentioned that Starr made prosecution decisions by a "committee of the whole."

Sol Wisenberg described it to investigators as "flat, open . . . in retrospect, too open."

Bruce Udolf characterized OIC as working like a "law school study group."

"[Michael] Emmick described the decision-making process as 'terribly unwieldy.' . . . [He] compared the activities in the office [to] an 'anthill,' stating that people were constantly flowing through the offices, in and out of meetings."

As Harris described to me earlier, "The captain of the ship does not consult with the crew on how to run the ship."

On the issue of whether Emmick was cleared by Starr to offer immunity, Emmick recalled, "As they were leaving the office [for the confrontation of Lewinsky] . . . [he] asked Starr, 'If it turns out we need to offer complete immunity, are the people there authorized to make the decision?' Starr replied that 'if it comes to that, people on-site must make the decision.'

"Starr stated he did not recall any further meeting before the attorneys left for the Ritz, but that he understands Emmick's recollection is different. Starr stated that he has no reason to believe Emmick's recollection is incorrect. . . . He stated that if Mike Emmick had come to him, he would have said yes because that was consistent with getting the facts quickly."

Regarding Lewinsky attorney Frank Carter: "Starr stated that at the time, they thought Lewinsky's attorney was complicit in the obstruction. . . . Specifically, he recalled the attorney's alleged suggestion to Lewinsky that she say, 'I don't recall.' In the context of their DC investigations and history of witnesses with little recollection, this was very troubling."

The phrase "I don't recall" implies that someone may or may not have personal knowledge of information regarding one or more conversations or events. Starr is suggesting that witnesses in the Clinton investigation with little recollection may not have been entirely truthful with OIC attorneys.

However, in one page from special counsels' interview, Starr did not recall thirteen times concerning details of two critical meetings with his deputies and Department of Justice attorney Josh Hochberg regarding the legal options available to OIC before contacting Lewinsky, as well as facts related to the brace.

In the entire interview, Starr does not recall or does not remember fifteen times. By comparison, Jackie Bennett could not recall or remember conversations or events ten times; Robert Bittman, nine; Michael Emmick, six; Bruce Udolf, five; Solomon Wisenberg, two; Sam Dash, none; Josh Hochberg, none; and Ken Starr, fifteen times—thirteen times regarding the Hochberg meetings and related facts, and two additional times: "specifics of [a] briefing," and "specific, precise statements" on the Tripp tapes, both reasonable lapses.

In the same interview, Ken Starr recalled, at length, his "deliberative process," his "collegial, nonhierarchical structure," "the job of the deputies," the handling of "prosecution memos"; he described "teams of lawyers assigned to various matters," the responsibilities of team leaders; he "cited the Denton matter" to Harris regarding contacting Lewinsky; and he "detailed the chronology of his involvement in the Lewinsky matter." Yet, when it comes to the details of two critical meetings with an attorney from the Public Integrity section of the department about contacting Lewinsky—an individual represented by an attorney and a key target in the Clinton investigation—Starr says he "does not recall" thirteen times.

To borrow special counsels' characterization of Starr's words, "This [is] very troubling."

More importantly, "Starr did not recall . . . any statement regarding a *Margolis* procedure."

But that's not how Josh Hochberg remembers it.

"Hochberg vividly recalls stating that if it were his case, he would not go forward without first contacting David Margolis. Hochberg explained to OIC that Margolis, who is an associate deputy attorney general in the Department of Justice, could give written authorization for the contacts when there was an issue."

Inside the department, Margolis "was regarded...as an all-knowing, Yoda-like figure," *The New York Times* wrote. "Deputy Attorney General Sally Yates called him 'the go-to guy for department leaders for over 50 years.'" Upon his death in 2016, James Comey, deputy attorney general at the time, said, "David Margolis *was* the United States Department of Justice."

Faced with the option of going to Margolis for his legal expertise, as Hochberg suggested, "Starr replied that Mike Emmick had looked at the issue; he knew the ethics rule and had concluded it was okay.

"During this meeting, Hochberg recalls that he was still uncomfortable regarding the contacts issue and remembers that Starr said, 'We don't consider her represented for these purposes.' Hochberg said he still had some discomfort."

As the Hochberg interview indicates, Starr was engaged in the discussion even as the independent counsel chose not to avail himself of the means that would have removed any question regarding how OIC contacted Lewinsky.

As to the reliability of Josh Hochberg's memory, the deputy chief from the Public Integrity section of the department memorialized his meetings with OIC in fifteen pages of notes that he provided Harris and Harkenrider at the time of his interview, as well as a three-page, internal Office of Professional Responsibility report summarizing the conversations between OIC and himself.

After discovering an entry for Starr's handwritten notes in the DC manifest, I contacted Reed at the archives and added them to a list of documents, specifically January through July 1998, the time frame of the Secret Service matter. However, the only months he could locate from that period were March, April, May, and July.

In April and May, OIC was focused on the Lewinsky issue and breaking through the legal barriers in getting Secret Service agents to testify about what they may have seen or heard regarding Clinton and Lewinsky's intimate relationship. Although many of Starr's notes focus on legal details, strategies, and conversations with his prosecutors, some notes reference conversations and meetings with other Republicans.

In April, Starr records:

"Frank Keating—4/22/98—is willing to sign a letter; [indistinct] contact others in that position."

Keating's name appears a second time on the same page:

"This week—Frank Keating."

In early May, Starr notes:

"—Had lunch with Frank Keating in Okla. City at the Gov's mansion."

Although it is unclear what the letter was about, or whom the others were, Starr's interactions with Governor Keating confirmed what a source told me earlier when they said that Starr was talking to "Frank Keating, about every other day. . . . He's . . . the lead prosecutor investigating the president of the United States. Why is he talking to Frank Keating?"

During the Reagan administration, Frank Keating was assistant Treasury secretary, the cabinet department that oversaw the Secret Service. In mid-May, Keating told *Washington Post* reporter Peter Baker, "Agents should not be talking about purely private matters in purely private situations."

Why did Ken Starr have so many conversations with Keating? Was he looking for a pathway to obtaining agent testimony? And based on his statement to Baker, did Keating effectively shut the door on the issue with Starr?

I had several questions for Judge Starr about the nature of his conversations with Governor Keating, but again, he declined to be interviewed. Despite reaching out to three organizations, I could not contact Keating.

However, Keating wasn't the only consultant to the independent counsel.

The source recalled attending a meeting with David Bossie, a Republican congressman hired by Dan Burton as chief investigator of Clinton. Walking into the office, the source and a colleague were surprised by what they saw.

"They had a chart up in the office with maybe fifty suspects, and they all had an international red circle with no slash through it. One was Hillary. They were all people who worked for Clinton: Vince Foster, Web Hubble. I remember there was so much hate in that room."

"Why were you in Burton's office?"

"They were funneling info to us. We can't give grand jury information, but we can *receive* information. Now, whether information was flowing to them, I have no knowledge. Nobody told me. I wouldn't go along with that if it happened."

When it comes to hypocrisy and bombast, Dan Burton, the formidable head of the House Committee on Government Reform and Oversight, was notorious in Capitol Hill lore.

In a December 1998 *Salon* story, "Portrait of a Political 'Pit Bull,'" Russ Baker points out that the Indiana Republican who consistently railed against the moral outrages of Bill Clinton, the man who allegedly groped a female lobbyist from Planned Parenthood, the representative who received a 100 percent rating from the Christian Coalition, admitted to an affair he had in the early '80s, resulting in an illegitimate son. However, it was Burton who outed himself, not out of any moral angst but because *Vanity Fair* was set to release a detailed story about him. It was Burton who alleged that Vince Foster, deputy White House counsel, had been murdered, even as he regaled his House colleagues in 1994 with an hour-long speech spreading a conspiracy theory that three investigations had disproved. A Senate Banking Committee came to the same conclusion a year later.

Now, Burton and Bossie were apparently part of the team investigating Clinton.

"We were in the room with these guys, meeting with an investigator," the source said. "I'd seen him on TV, one of those conservative talking heads; [Bossie] was a chief investigator. I don't remember what we talked about, but I remember there was so much cross-pollination with these political figures."

A May 6 entry in Starr's notes describes a phone call from Burton: "I just called to give you encouragement. My admiration for you has grown 200%, 300%, and it was already high. You've been subjected to vilification. So have I. You are doing the Lord's work."

Regarding her work as special counsel, I asked Jo Ann Harris, "When you say you were independent, you were independent even from the Office of Professional Responsibility knowing exactly what you were doing, is that correct?"

"Yes," Harris said. "I would not have taken the job if I didn't have assurances of *complete* independence."

"Did you ever have the feeling that anyone was intruding on your investigation who should not have done so?"

"No. They wouldn't dare," Harris said unequivocally.

"I assume you would have reported such conduct."

"Yes."

Why was Ken Starr talking to two Republican politicians during his investigation, and what other individuals was he speaking with during that time? Is it normal for an independent counsel to meet or speak with partisans during a high-profile investigation of the president of the United States?

From May 11 to 14, Starr writes that he is preparing for the Secret Service argument before the court. He describes comments by his deputy, Bob Bittman.

Bob Points—

—I was shocked by Lew Merletti's comment in not [recognizing] the privilege would lead to another assassination.

Ps [presidents] have kept agents at some distance, for a variety of reasons.

—Lew M. was the personal choice of the Clintons. He was probably the best choice.

That last comment suggests a relationship between Merletti and Clinton beyond that of agent and president, the same "special relationship" that Solomon Wisenberg believed existed.

In March, Starr records this series of notes:

Secret Service

    (i)   Sam Dash—Consult

    (ii)   Mike Shaheen—Consult

    (iii)   Litigation team—Meet

    (iv)   Jackie . . . quality of source info.

Shaheen was the first director of DOJ's Office of Professional Responsibility and held the post until 1997. He investigated government corruption and was quick to point out "perceived ethical lapses by the nation's highest officials," *The New York Times* reported. However, that last entry, underlined, could be a reference to OIC's source inside the Secret Service. The notation suggests that Starr was preparing to question deputy Jackie Bennett concerning the authenticity or corroboration of the source's information. As Bittman recalled in our interview, "My memory was that the source came to Jackie."

On the first page of Starr's notes from July, I found two notations that appeared to stress the importance of getting more information from Lewinsky and the Secret Service.

Associate independent counsel Mark Barrett comments to Starr: "*This would be a live grenade. Do it right. Monica Lewinsky + Secret Service.*"

Ken Starr agreed: "*We need Monica or Secret Service.*"

Based on their urgency, and notations marked July 14 that appear ten pages later, it seems that these notes were written before Supreme Court Justice Rehnquist ruled on July 17 that agents must testify.

In the four months of Starr's notes that cover the time frame of the Secret Service matter that I examined, he mentions the Secret Service, agents, and the "protective function" privilege seventy times; Director Merletti, five times.

However, what's conspicuously missing from Starr's written record are the months of January, February, and June.

January 1998 was when OIC likely received word from their source about a deal between Merletti and Clinton. They also received two pages faxed to the Washington office from Little Rock on the 29th: a memo from the Association of Former Agents of the US Secret Service regarding the release of the Hersh book on Kennedy, *The Dark Side of Camelot*, and Merletti's directive about agents remaining silent regarding the conversations of protectees; and a second page on "how to find people" who come and go from the White House, Secret Service shift reports, and the Uniformed Division's gate log. However, there was no written reaction to any of this information from Starr nor did he record any comments from his deputies because the National Archives had no notes from Ken Starr for January.

February 1998 was when Director Merletti gave his first presentation to Starr and Bittman regarding protection. Although Bittman did discuss Merletti's presentation in my interview, there were no notes that record Starr's or Bittman's reaction to Merletti's first presentation or a second a few days later with department officials present. Even an internal OIC memo documenting a timeline of the Secret Service matter lists the first meeting. There were no notes by Starr recording Merletti's reaction to hearing their source's allegation that he helped facilitate the Clinton/ Lewinsky relationship and no notes on any attempts to corroborate the allegation because the archives had no notes from Starr for February.

In June 1998, five OIC attorneys and Ken Starr, received the Deep Throat letter via the Little Rock office. No notes referencing Deep

Throat; no copy of the Deep Throat letter in Starr's work files; no reaction from the five other attorneys who received the letter; and no notes regarding corroboration of the source because the archives had no notes from Starr for June.

I did locate and read notes from December 1997, one month before the Secret Service matter had begun, and August 1998, one month after the matter had been settled by Chief Justice Rehnquist. They contained no mention of Deep Throat or "source." Other months were missing as well.

Reading 311 pages of handwritten notes left me with the impression that Ken Starr was a man who kept a detailed record of his thoughts, strategies, questions, "to do" lists, calendars, comments from his staff, numerous reactions from journalists, ("He was obsessed with public relations," a source told Sidney Blumenthal), even conversations and meetings with other Republicans. Yet, when it came to an anonymous source inside the Secret Service that he, Bittman, Wisenberg, and Bennett steadfastly believed, who alleged collusion between President Clinton and Secret Service Director Merletti, I could not locate any notes from Starr regarding the authenticity, corroboration, or even a mention of a source.

Again, the Federal Records Act of 1950 directs the preservation of those records necessary to document federal activities.

In the letter I received from a former associate independent counsel, he wrote, "When we left OIC we were instructed to leave all OIC material."

If the staff was instructed to leave all material, what happened to the notes missing from Ken Starr's handwritten record of Merletti's two presentations? Given his penchant for regular note-taking, it seems unusual that Starr would not record any details about a source inside the Secret Service.

In his book *Contempt: A Memoir of the Clinton Investigation*, Starr is sharp in his critique of the "protective function" privilege as a defense against having agents testify about the president's personal life.

Starr writes, "frivolous . . . novel idea . . . bizarre notion . . . heretical doctrine . . . cleverly invented . . . bogus . . . ginned-up.

"The Solicitor General's office helped block the subpoenas," Starr writes. "The president was now advancing through the formal apparatus of DOJ a dubious constitutional doctrine animated entirely by self-interest, for individual, not institutional, reasons."

There are several issues to unpack from Starr's claims. First and foremost is the suggestion that solicitor general Seth Waxman, DOJ officials, Treasury officials, four former Secret Service directors, and twelve individuals in an Amicus brief, may have been part of a scheme to obstruct the Office of Independent Counsel in its investigation.

Although the privilege Director Merletti and DOJ sought had no basis in current law, they argued that agents should not be asked to testify about the conversations and actions of a protectee. When it comes to criminal matters, however, their duty *requires* reporting to both the Secret Service director as well as the secretary of the Treasury, under which the Secret Service was attached. (It is currently under the Department of Homeland Security.)

Contrary to what Mr. Starr and his prosecutors believed, the privilege was not "bogus" or "heretical." Rather, it stemmed from and was consistent with current laws that permit doctor–patient, priest–penitent, and attorney–client confidentiality.

Nor was the privilege "cleverly invented."

As noted by Judge Susan Webber Wright in *Jones v. Clinton*, without a "protective function" privilege, Secret Service testimony "could possibly provide critical information at the core of how the Secret Service actually functions and provide those with hostile intent toward the President with important information to use in piercing the Secret Service's protection."

Merletti made his case through the same presentation to Starr that he made to Janet Reno whom Harris described as "absolutely dedicated to doing the right thing," and the entire upper echelon of the department, as well as Solicitor General Seth Waxman, who was no pushover.

It was not, as Starr writes, for "self-interest" by Clinton but to defend the institutional protective mandate of the Secret Service, and previous written statements made by past directors regarding personal privacy as far back as 1910 support Merletti's position.

All this evidence was brought out not only in Merletti's presentation to Starr but also through supportive documents of past directors, as well as a letter from former president George H. W. Bush.

The only compelling evidence Starr and OIC had appeared to be from one anonymous source, Deep Throat, an individual who would not go on the record and whose claims the independent counsel could not corroborate.

Moreover, Starr doesn't even mention the Deep Throat source in his memoir. He doesn't reference the letter, nor does he talk about his attempts to substantiate the allegations by the source. To read Ken Starr's book, he never *heard* of Lewis Merletti—the principal actor in OIC's Secret Service collusion theory—because, despite numerous references in OIC files, including Starr's handwritten notes, he also is not mentioned in the book.

To borrow Special Counsel Harris's words regarding the false complicity notion of Lewinsky attorney Frank Carter, there was little evidentiary basis for concluding that Merletti was involved in any deal with Clinton.

"Based on the available evidence," journalist Bob Woodward concluded in 1999, "[Clinton] confided in no one and conspired with no one."

Lastly, Starr himself said as much in his phone call to Merletti's office at the end of the investigation: "The Secret Service was a dry hole. You knew nothing."

Again, not mentioned in the book.

In media interviews during his investigation, Starr insisted, "We want the truth. We want all the truth. We want it completely, accurately."

It appears Judge Starr did not live up to his own standard. Rather, he seems to confirm what Harris told me: "He can talk about the truth all he wants, but he is, from what I can see, a very self-righteous person who really has no clue as to how to exercise judgment in very complicated situations."

Near the end of his book, Starr references part of John Adams's well-known quote made before a jury in defense of British soldiers accused in the Boston Massacre: "Facts are stubborn things."

However, he neglects the critical words that precede that wisdom: "and whatever may be our wishes, our inclinations, or the dictates of our passion, they cannot alter the state of facts and evidence."

Do I believe Bill Clinton lied regarding several matters before the independent counsel?

You bet!

However, I also believe that Starr and his prosecutors allowed their wishes, their inclinations, and the dictates of their passion to override good, objective practice regarding the Lewinsky and Secret Service matters, and were willing to do whatever was necessary to bring an indictment against the president of the United States.

Furthermore, by appearing before the House Judiciary Committee regarding his advocacy for impeachment, Ken Starr violated his obligations as independent counsel, unlawfully intruded, and abused the powers of his office.

That's not *my* judgment. That's the judgment of Starr's own ethics advisor, Sam Dash. In Robert Ray's *Final Report of the Independent Counsel* is a letter of resignation from Dash addressed to Ken Starr.

Dated November 20, 1998, Dash begins by praising Starr:
I found that you conducted yourself with integrity and professionalism.

Dash then proceeds to do a complete one-eighty:
I resign for a fundamental reason. Against my strong advice, you decided to depart from your usual professional decision-making by accepting the invitation of the House Judiciary Committee to appear before the committee and serve as an aggressive advocate for the proposition that the evidence in your referral demonstrates that the President committed impeachable offenses. In doing this you have violated your obligations under the Independent Counsel Statute and have unlawfully intruded on the power of impeachment which the Constitution gives solely to the House. As Independent Counsel, you have only one narrow duty under the statute relating to the House's power of impeachment. That one

duty . . . of the statute, is to objectively provide for the House substantial and credible information that may constitute grounds for impeachment.

The statute does not and could not constitutionally give the Independent Counsel any role in impeachment other than this single informing function. . . .

Frequently, you have publicly stated that you have sought my advice in major decisions and had my approval. I cannot allow that inference to continue regarding your present abuse of your office and have no other choice but to resign.

Notwithstanding Dash's earlier praise, the man known as the father of the Independent Counsel Statute makes clear that Ken Starr "violated [his] obligations . . . unlawfully intruded . . . and abuse[d] [his] office."

However, Dash's resignation letter was written two years *before* learning additional information from Special Counsels Harris and Harkenrider during his May 16, 2000, interview, where his judgment regarding the confrontation of Lewinsky decidedly changed.

"Dash was not informed that Lewinsky was told that the value of her cooperation would be less if she called Frank Carter. Nor was Dash informed that Lewinsky was told by agents and/or attorneys that OIC would tell her attorney as much as they would tell her. Dash never saw the 302 recounting Lewinsky's desire for the agents to 'talk to [my] lawyer.' Dash indicated that all of these statements, if made, would have been relevant to his analysis. Dash stated that if he thought 'they sought to dissuade her from representation,' he would have been very troubled."

If Sam Dash had been given this information after OIC confronted Lewinsky, one wonders if he would have resigned sooner.

Robert Ray's *Final Report* was released to the public on March 6, 2002.

While Ray states that the Secret Service "protective function" privilege was rejected by the courts and agents were required to testify, there is no mention of their Deep Throat source, corroboration of or lack thereof. There is no statement from the January 18, 2001 meeting where Merletti was interviewed prior to a grand jury appearance that was cancelled. And no conclusion referencing my source's statement that "We all walked away with the opinion that [Merletti] was a very credible person. And . . . if he wasn't called before the grand jury, it was because there was a decision made that, 'Hey, there was no collusion here. Why are we wasting our time?'"

In a televised statement that also appears on the first page of Robert Ray's *Final Report of the Independent Counsel,* I found one piece of text by Ray to be particularly ironic: "I have tried to heed Justice Robert Jackson's wisdom:

> The citizen's safety lies in the prosecutor who tempers zeal with
> human kindness, who seeks truth and not victims, who serves
> the law and not factional purposes, and who approaches his
> task with humility.

They weren't kind. Lewinsky, Merletti and the Secret Service became victims. They appeared to serve partisan purposes in their contact with other Republicans, and they lacked humility in the process.

Owing to his lack of experience as a federal prosecutor and overreliance on his staff, the independent counsel's fatal flaw was assumption. Starr assumed that Lewinsky attorney Frank Carter was complicit in the deception to lie about the relationship between Clinton and Lewinsky. Starr assumed that he didn't need to consult with Sam Dash on the ethical issues surrounding the brace of Lewinsky *before* she was confronted at the Ritz-Carlton even though he was brought into the office by Starr specifically to consult on such issues. Starr assumed that his Deep Throat source inside the Secret Service was genuine despite no confirmatory evidence. He assumed that Merletti's memo to agents about confidentiality issued before the Lewinsky matter was known was an attempt to pre-emptively restrain agent testimony to the independent counsel. He assumed that Merletti's appointment to Secret Service director appeared to be evidence that Merletti had a deal with Clinton. And he assumed that bringing all prosecutors to the table by way of his "deliberative process [and] committee of the whole" would result in more effective decision-making.

One could argue that Ken Starr was a victim of his own investigation. He was "an academic, brilliant law guy," Harris described, "and the worst possible kind of person you should put in charge of an independent counsel's office."

Sam Dash's assessment was harsher. "He lacked the judgment, even the understanding of the role of a federal prosecutor. So he delegated to these very aggressive prosecutors."

Starr himself points out his weaknesses. "Fiske's sweeping investigative focus . . . was nowhere near my professional sweet spot."

And his style as OIC's chief was to examine the legal aspects, then discuss with his staff before making many decisions by consensus.

Ultimately, the Lewinsky matter cost Ken Starr and his office the loss of their reputations. In a CBS News/*New York Times* poll asking if Ken Starr's investigation was "impartial" or "partisan," only 27 percent believed it was "impartial," whereas 64 percent believed it to be "partisan." The same poll asked respondents if they thought the time, effort, and money spent on the independent counsel's investigation was worth it. Seventy-eight percent believed it was "not worth it."

Five days after the Rehnquist decision compelling agent testimony, another CBS News/*New York Times* poll asked, "Should Secret Service agents testify?" Fifty-eight percent of respondents selected "No."

The same poll asked, "Does testimony interfere with protection?" Forty-eight percent of respondents selected "Yes, seriously."

When the Office of Independent Counsel proceedings finally closed, no charges had been brought against Bill and Hillary Clinton in the Whitewater investigation. Robert Ray "determined that the evidence was insufficient to prove to a jury beyond a reasonable doubt that either [the] president or Mrs. Clinton knowingly participated in any criminal conduct."

In one of my final interviews with Jo Ann Harris, she observed, "My fundamental concern here is that a prosecutor's office has more power and more responsibility in our criminal justice system to see that it is fair and just. And that the public has confidence that it is fair and just. I think that Starr's whole operation was sort of the 'poster boy' for causing a lack of public confidence in what prosecutors do."

On the day Bill Clinton's impeachment trial was due to end, Constitutional scholar Laurence Tribe wrote these words in a *New York Times* opinion piece that sound eerily prophetic:

> Although some will continue to condemn an acquittal of this President as proof that no Constitution, however brilliantly conceived, can protect us from our own moral weakness, I believe history is more likely to view it as a verdict that kept the Constitution's processes of impeachment and removal intact

so that they might serve their crucial mission if and when we face a genuine threat of tyranny.

Epilogue

Standing before the attendees at the FBI National Academy on Ethics and Leadership conference in Cleveland on March 2000, Merletti directed his final remarks at Ken Starr.

The Secret Service is decidedly nonpartisan and nonpolitical. The training and daily operations of Secret Service personnel transcend political party or crisis of the moment. This was not about President Clinton, but about the office of the Presidency and the Secret Service's ability to protect it, now and in the future. Assassination jeopardizes the National Security of the United States; it jeopardizes the security of the American people. The independent counsel has *never* and will *never* have to shoulder the responsibility of protecting the office of the Presidency.

Our argument for a privilege is new because the Secret Service was never forced to testify before

Not during the special prosecutor's investigation of Watergate during the Nixon administration.

Not during the investigation of Vice President Agnew for tax fraud.

Not during the independent counsel investigation of President Reagan and Vice President Bush during Iran Contra.

The independent counsel continued in his insistence on our testimony. He stood on case law. The Secret Service agents who have covered our American presidents with their own flesh and blood during assassination attempts were not doing it to meet requirements of case law. They were doing it to meet their commitment to duty.

In the United States Secret Service, we live by an unwritten code, an invisible web of obligation to those who have gone before us. We would sooner die than fail. That is not rhetoric, it is our commitment to our nation.

We live in a dangerous world where the national security of the United States is constantly tested and challenged, and where our national character is defined in terms of sacrifice and commitment. Secret Service history has proven that confidentiality affords us the proximity that is critical to the success of our mission. *Proximity* is the difference between life and death to our protectees.

My experience has taught me that in crucial moments, you lead not by avoiding issues, or shouting or delegating, but rather by meeting issues head-on; standing up for the values we hold so dear; the beliefs we treasure, and the ethics to which we are committed.

Duty, honor, courage, commitment: these intangibles are our strengths. They prevail over darkness, time and time again. I urge you to stand up for these values. They are the bedrock principles to which we are committed.

The independent counsel's office was so caught up in their own narrow interest of the moment that they lost sight of future consequences. If history teaches us anything, it is that there can be no justice without restraint. The end does not justify the means.

After an examination of independent counsel investigations concerning the Iran Contra and Whitewater/Lewinsky matters, both parties in Congress concluded that the law had become too susceptible to overreach and allowed the act to lapse in 1999 leading the Department of Justice to establish the Office of Special Counsel.

Congress has not passed legislation for a confidentiality privilege, leaving the Secret Service vulnerable to future investigations.

After Merletti's battle with the independent counsel ended, the Secret Service remained distanced from politics . . . until Donald Trump.

Acknowledgments

Based on 12 years of research, *Trust and Confidence* is the best available evidence concerning the Monica Lewinsky and Secret Service matters.

I am grateful to all those who contributed to my understanding of a story that has largely gone unreported.

I am especially indebted to Lewis Merletti, former director of the US Secret Service, whose character had been tested and, despite the personal consequences, chose to stand on principle during a toxic political crisis.

Kat Mathis, Merletti's executive assistant, was always available, from tracking down dates from his calendars as director to many documents from his files.

The Office of Special Counsel

Jo Ann Harris, former head of the criminal division at the Department of Justice, was unquestionably important in detailing her special counsel investigation over several years. Before her untimely death, she reviewed virtually all my work. Her integrity and tenacity in sticking to the standards of the Office of Professional Responsibility and sticking by me made a difficult path much clearer: many phone calls; many questions; and Jo Ann answered them all with knowledge, and insight. She and her co-counsel, Mary Frances Harkenrider, are role models for Justice attorneys.

The National Archives and Records Administration

I am deeply grateful to Robert Reed, Archivist extraordinaire. I would never have been able to gather and write such a complete and detailed account of the Lewinsky and Secret Service matters without his help. Rob's focus, skill, and persistence on my behalf were invaluable.

The Office of the Independent Counsel

Robert J. Bittman, deputy independent counsel; Solomon L. Wisenberg, deputy independent counsel; Michael Emmick, associate independent counsel; Bruce Udolf, associate independent counsel; Rodger Heaton, associate independent counsel; and Paul S. Rosenzweig, senior litigation counsel. While some conversations may have been a bit rocky, I appreciate their time. All my questions were aimed at finding the most accurate account of events.

The Department of Justice

Kenneth Courter, Acting Chief, FOIA/Privacy Act Unit, Office of Enforcement Operations, Criminal Division, US Department of Justice. After six unproductive months searching for the special counsel's report,

Ken helped speed the process along until I located Harris's report in the National Archives.

And the others who contributed:

Cynthia Summerfelt, Special Assistant, FOIA/PA Unit, Office of Enforcement Operations, Criminal Division, US Department of Justice; Louis Sims, former US Secret Service Agent during the Nixon Administration; Bryant Johnson, Public Operations Supervisor, United States District Court for the District of Columbia; Joe Martin, US Court of Appeals, District of Columbia Circuit; Marilyn R. Sargent, Chief Deputy Clerk, US Court of Appeals; Martha Wagner Murphy, Chief, Special Access and FOIA, National Archives at College Park; and Myles "Chappy" Mattenson, an uncommon attorney and friend.

Finally . . .

To Caren, who never once asked, "Are you finished, yet? When will it be finished?" This project would have been impossible without her *unconditional* support.

Bibliography

Trust and Confidence is based on personal interviews; documents from the personal files of former Secret Service director Lewis Merletti; *The Referral from Independent Counsel Kenneth W. Starr in Conformity with the Requirement of Title 28, United States Code, § Section 595(c)*, from the Office of Independent Counsel, Kenneth W. Starr, September 9, 1998; *The Report of the Special Counsel Concerning Allegations of Professional Misconduct by the Office of Independent Counsel in Connection with the Encounter with Monica Lewinsky on January 16, 1998*, by special counsels Jo Ann Harris and Mary Frances Harkenrider, December 6, 2000; the *Final Report of the Independent Counsel: In Re: Madison Guaranty Savings & Loan Association/Regarding Monica Lewinsky and Others*, by Robert W. Ray, March 6, 2002; "The WACO Hearings," joint congressional subcommittee, July 20, 1995; documents from the Kenneth Starr/Robert Ray/Julie Thomas records of the Office of Independent Counsel retained at the National Archives and Records Administration; and news accounts from 1998.

Jim Lichtman

Books

Blaine, Gerald, and Lisa McCubbin. *The Kennedy Detail: JFK's Secret Service Agents Break Their Silence*. New York: Gallery Books, 2010.

Blumenthal, Sidney, *The Clinton Wars*. New York: Farrar, Straus and Giroux, 2003.

Fiske, Jr., Robert B., *Prosecutor, Defender, Counselor – The Memoirs of Robert B. Fiske, Jr..* Kittery, ME: Smith/Kerr Associates LLC, 2014.

Freeh, Louis J., with Howard Means. *My FBI – Bringing Down the Mafia, Investigating Bill Clinton, and Fighting the War on Terror*. New York: St. Martin's Press, 2005.

Gormley, Ken. *The Death of American Virtue: Clinton vs. Starr.* New York: Crown Publishers, 2010.

Hersh, Seymour M. *The Dark Side of Camelot*. New York: Little Brown, 1997.

Kessler, Ronald. *In the President's Secret Service.* New York: Crown, 2009.

Kuntz, Phil, ed. *The Starr Report: The Evidence.* New York: Pocket Books, 1998.

Lichtman, Jim. *What Do You Stand For?* Palm Desert, CA: Scribbler's Ink, 2004.

Melanson, Philip H. *The Secret Service: The Hidden History of an Enigmatic Agency.* New York: Basic Books, 2005.

Melanson, Philip H. *The Secret Service: The Hidden History of an Enigmatic Agency.* New York: Basic Books, 2002.

Petro, Joseph, with Jeffrey Robinson. *Standing Next to History*. New York: Thomas Dunne Books/St. Martin's Press, 2005.

Ray, Robert W. *Final Report of the Independent Counsel: In Re: Madison Guaranty Savings & Loan Association Regarding Monica Lewinsky and Others, March 6, 2002.*

Schmidt, Susan, and Michael Weisskopf. *Truth at Any Cost: Ken Starr and the Unmaking of Bill Clinton*. New York: Perennial, 2000.

Starr, Ken. *Contempt: A Memoir of the Clinton Investigation*. New York: Sentinel, 2018.

Starr, Kenneth W. *Referral from Independent Counsel Kenneth W. Starr in Conformity with the Requirements of Title 28, United States Code, § Section 595(c)*. Washington, DC: US Government Printing Office, 1998.

Woodward, Bob. *Shadow: Five Presidents and the Legacy of Watergate*. New York: Simon & Schuster; 1999.

Woodward, Bob. *The Secret Man* New York: Simon & Schuster, 2005.

Scholarly Paper

Harris, Jo Ann. *The Federal Independent Counsel Act*, [an unpublished work], Notes for Faculty Colloquium Presentation, Elisabeth Haub School of Law at Pace University, New York, May 1996. Used with permission of the author.

Media

The Waco Investigation Day 2, Part 3, C-SPAN Videotape 66317-1, part 1 of 2, July 20, 1995.

The Waco Investigation Day 4, Part 1, C-SPAN Videotape 66308-1, part 1 of 2, July 24, 1995.

The Waco Investigation Day 4, Part 1, C-SPAN Videotape 66308-1, part 2 of 2, July 24, 1995

"National Academy (FBI) 'Leadership' conference; speech by Lewis C. Merletti, March 30, 2000.

Source Notes

Prologue

Page 1: "The way I'm going to tell you this": Merletti interview, November 7, 2007.

2: "'BEING WORTHY OF TRUST AND CONFIDENCE'": "Declaration of Lewis C. Merletti, Director, United States Secret Service," Justice Department court filing, April 21, 1998, p. 15, section 22, Merletti files.

Chapter 1

5: "Merletti was preparing to speak to an audience of FBI agents": Merletti interview, November 7, 2007.

5: "We wanted to be the first to meet you, sir": Ibid.

6: "Whitewater scandal has its genesis": Jeff Gerth, "The 1992 Campaign: Personal Finances; Clintons Joined S.&L. Operator in an Ozark Real Estate Venture," *New York Times*, March 8,

1992,   https://www.nytimes.com/1992/03/08/us/1992-campaign-personal-finances-clintons-joined-s-l-operator-ozark-real-estate.html?searchResultPosition=1

6: "After several criminal referrals by RTC to the Department of Justice.": Fiske, Jr., Robert B., *Prosecutor Defender Counselor – The Memoirs of Robert B. Fiske, Jr..* (Kittery, ME: Smith/Kerr Associates LLC, 2014), p. 232.

6: "as the regulatory independent counsel": *The Federal Independent Counsel Act,* by Jo Ann Harris, Scholar in Residence, Elisabeth Haub School of Law at Pace University, New York, May 1996, an unpublished work, p. 2.

As Harris describes, the Independent Counsel Statute had expired, "Fiske was named under a long-existing regulation under which the AG can appoint, as a special employee of DOJ, an independent counsel."

6: "Special Division of the Court of Appeals for the District of Columbia. The judges were selected by William Rehnquist, the Chief Justice of the Supreme Court": Ibid. p. 5.

7: "William P. Barr removed Geoffrey S. Berman": Barbara Campbell, Ryan Lucas, Colin Dwyer, and Jason Slotkin, "President Trump Fires Top US Prosecutor Who Investigates His Allies, Barr Says," National Public Radio, June 20, 2020.

Washington   Post,   https://www.washingtonpost.com/politics/geoffrey-berman-us-attorney-william-barr-trump/2020/06/20/fcbfa3b4-b30f-11ea-8758-bfd1d045525a_story.html

7: "After a nineteen-month Freedom of Information Act (FOIA) request": Author's FOIA request addressed to Rena Y. Kim at FOIA, Department of Justice (DOJ), October 25, 2011; follow-up with Ken Courter at FOIA/DOJ by phone, May 1, 2013; referred to Gary Stern at the National Archives and Records Administration (NARA); referred to Martha Wagner Murphy, chief of special access and FOIA staff, May 15, 2013.

8: "When Tripp made that phone call": Harris interview, June 26, 2014.

8: "My life lessons go back to 1967": Merletti response to questionnaire, March 1, 1999: Jim Lichtman, *What Do You Stand For?* (Palm Desert, CA: Scribbler's Ink, 2004), p. 85.

10: "I received your letter dated May 4, 1999": Response letter from Merletti, May 7, 1999.

11: "This was the most painful period of my life": Merletti phone conversation, approximately May 10, 1999.

Chapter 2

14: "Our chief counsel, John Kelleher": Merletti interview, November 7, 2007.

15: "Mr. Merletti, this office has the highest respect for the Secret Service": Ibid.

17: "He had some type of information," Merletti said, "some 'Deep Throat' type of information": Ibid.

17: "Reviewing everything Felt said to me, it is apparent he was wrong on a number of things.": Bob Woodward, *The Secret Man* (New York: Simon & Schuster, 2005), p. 76.

18: "Starr's investigators spent weeks": Susan Schmidt and Michael Weisskopf, *Truth at Any Cost* (New York: HarperCollins, 2000), p. 137.

18: "The tip came from a source connected to the Secret Service's top command": Ibid., p. 32.

18: "[Starr] spent weeks ... hundreds and hundreds of man-hours": Merletti interview, November 7, 2007.

19: "The normally placid Holder": Susan Schmidt and Michael Weisskopf, *Truth at Any Cost*, p. 143.

19: "That's putting it mildly": Merletti interview, November 7, 2007.

19: "The Secret Service director had just learned": Susan Schmidt and Michael Weisskopf, *Truth at Any Cost*, p. 143.

19: "My predecessor, Eljay Bowron": Merletti interview, November 7, 2007.

21: "'Merletti did this whole thing,' an agent pushed the former director": Ibid.

21: "Doesn't surprise me": Harris phone conversation, June 2014.

21: "Who do these FBI agents and Ken Starr think they are?": Merletti interview, November 7, 2007.

Chapter 3

23: "Merletti sat before a joint House subcommittee": "The Waco Hearings, Day 2, Part 3," C-SPAN, July 20, 1995, https://www.c-span.org/video/?66317-1/waco-investigation-day-2-part-3.

24: "gunshot wounds apparently inflicted by fellow cult members": *Report of the Department of the Treasury on the Bureau of Alcohol, Tobacco and Firearms Investigation of Vernon Wayne Howell also known as David Koresh*, September 1983, p. 1, https://archive.org/details/Reportofdepartme00unit/page/n7/mode/2up.

24: "I'm transferring you out of Baltimore": Merletti interview, November 7, 2007.

25: "He's making accusations that this report was unfair, biased, and a cover-up": The Waco Hearings, Day 2, Part 3, July 20, 1995.

28: "'I have *sixty-one witnesses* that said they heard that'": Ibid.

28: "'What was absolutely clear in Washington at Treasury and in Washington at ATF,' Noble said": *60 Minutes*, May 14, 1995, as reported in *The Los Angeles Times*, July 25, 1995.

28: "'Man, this guy didn't take any guff'": Merletti interview, November 7, 2007.

29: "I wish that I would have been able to tell all their stories": The Waco Hearings, Day 2, Part 3, July 20, 1995.

29: "One of the young men that was killed . . . Rob Williams": Ibid.

30: "Sorry," Merletti told Clinton, "it's about the truth": Merletti interview, November 7, 2007.

30: "This is not an all-volunteer army": Ibid.

Chapter 4

31: "Hey, there's a Republican here": Merletti interview, November 7, 2007.

31: "Frank Eugene Corder": "List of White House Security Breaches," Wikipedia, [Access date: 09-07-21], https://en.wikipedia.org/wiki/List_of_White_House_security_breaches.

31: "Francisco Martin Duran": Ibid.

32: "Marcelino Corniel": Merletti speech before the FBI National Academy, March 30, 2000, p. 6, Merletti files.

32: "William Modjeski": Ibid.

32: "In November 1996, a more calculated attack was directed at Clinton": Merletti phone conversation, sometime early 2008.

33: "I'm going to recommend you": Merletti interview, November 7, 2007.

Chapter 5

35: "She was in trouble": Jo Ann Harris and Mary Francis Harkenrider, *Report of the Special Counsel Concerning Allegations of Professional Misconduct by the Office of Independent Counsel in Connection with the Encounters with Monica Lewinsky on January 16, 1998*, December 6, 2000, Office of Special Counsel, (OSC) files within the Starr, Ray, Thomas Office of Independent Counsel (OIC) files, National Archives and Records Administration (NARA), p. 35.

37: "The minute she says, 'Can I call my lawyer?' you stop": Ken Gormley, *The Death of American Virtue* (New York: Crown, 2010), p. 674.

37: "The two had worked together for four years when tenured at the US Attorney's office in Southern District of New York": derived from Fiske, Jr., Robert B., *Prosecutor Defender Counselor – The Memoirs of Robert B. Fiske, Jr.* (Kittery, ME: Smith/Kerr Associates LLC, 2014), p. 222.

37: "Harris described Fiske as having a 'reputation for fairness, for toughness, for integrity'": Jo Ann Harris phone interview, September 16, 2012.

38: "About ten or twelve complaints were referred to OPR at the department": Ibid.

39: "I will be your OPR on this subject": Ibid.

39: "put both reports out there [Harris's report and Ray's rebuttal] and let the public decide": Ibid.

40: "Strongly adversarial substance and tone": OSC report, OSC/OIC files, NARA, p. 6.

40: "Due to the 'lack of a contemporaneous record'": Ibid, p. 7.

40: "Be independent and get it over with": Harris phone interview, September 16, 2012.

41: "No lawyer involved in the confrontation with Monica Lewinsky": OSC report, p. 2.

42: "Offering a Hobson's choice to Lewinsky": Ibid., p. 4.

42: "The doldrums at the Office of Independent Counsel were blown away": Ibid., p. 9.

42: "Viewed as an 'attack dog'": Francis X. Clines, "Starr Aide Is Seen as 'Attack Dog' or Tough Lawyer," *New York Times*, June 22, 1998, https://www.nytimes.com/1998/06/22/us/starr-aide-seen-as-attack-dog-or-tough-lawyer.html?searchResultPosition=1

42: "With Lewinsky, OIC had a potentially explosive witness": OSC report, OSC/OIC files, NARA, p. 10.

43: "'The issues were long of tooth'": Ibid., p. 9.

43: "Starr had no prosecuting experience": Ibid., p. 12.

44: "I really believe that many of the people appointed [independent counsels] are ill-suited for the job": Harris phone interview, September 16, 2012.

44: "The captain of the ship": Harris phone conversation, contemporaneous handwritten note on page 12, OSC report, sometime in May 2014.

45: "Starr hired prominent Washington lawyer and law professor Samuel Dash": OSC report, p. 13.

46: "this issue not only raised esoteric constitutional issues": Ibid., p. 17.

46: "run don't walk": Ibid., p. 18.

46: "The 1998 Martindale-Hubbell biography of Francis Carter": Ibid., p. 13.

46: "in DC, more people are convicted of covering up . . . You don't know who is friend, or foe; you can always come to me.": Ibid., p. 1.

46: "They approached her about a clear component of my representation": Jo Ann Harris and Mary Francis Harkenrider, "Memorandum of Interview," Frank Carter, June 6, 2000, OSC/OIC files, NARA, p. 2.

47: "The way in which Lewinsky ended up with Carter": OSC Report, p. 19, footnote 12.

47: "In Starr's words, it was their '*instinct* based upon experience with the Clinton people'": Ibid.

47: "Carter's character was 'unimpeachable'": Harris phone conversation, contemporaneous handwritten note on page 13, OSC report, sometime in May 2014.

47: "Robert Bittman . . . consulting by telephone acknowledged that they had information from Tripp that Lewinsky was misleading Carter": OSC report, p. 20, footnote 12.

48: "Breathing fire and brimstone": Jo Ann Harris and Mary Francis Harkenrider, "Memorandum of Interview," Kenneth W. Starr, June 23 and June 24, 2000, OSC files, p. 3.

48: "[Isikoff told OIC] that the White House was aware of inquiries about Lewinsky": OSC report, p. 20.

48: "Triage in analysis": Ibid., p. 20.

Chapter 6

49: "OIC staff began brainstorming": Office of Special Counsel (OSC) report, within the Starr, Ray, Thomas, Office of Independent Counsel (OIC) files, National Archives and Records Administration (NARA), p. 19.

49: "Known for his street-savvy": Viveca Novak, "Reno's Untouchables," *Time* magazine, May 19, 1997; Emily Langer, "Lee J. Radek, Former Chief of Justice Dept.'s Public Integrity, Dies at 69," *The Washington Post*, March 12, 2013, https://www.washingtonpost.com/local/obituaries/lee-j-radek-former-chief-of-justice-depts-spublic-integrity-section-dies-at-69/2013/03/12/cd6ff680-8a69-11e2-a051-6810d606108d_story.html.

50: "Hochberg suggested that if OIC had concerns about Carter's reliability or complicity'": OSC report, p. 22.

50: "*Margolis* procedure": Ibid.

50: "'Had a great deal of respect' for Hochberg": Jo Ann Harris and Mary Francis Harkenrider, "Memorandum of Interview," Kenneth W. Starr, June 23-24, 2000, OSC/OIC files, NARA, p. 4.

50: "'I was pretty confident [Bennett said]'": Harris and Harkenrider, "Memorandum of Interview," Jackie Bennett, June 22, 2000, OSC/OIC files, pp. 1–2.

51: "Starr . . . returned to the subject of jurisdiction": OSC report, p. 23.

51: "One, she's not represented here": Ibid., pp. 23–24.

52: "OIC's 'investigation was totally entwined with my representation'": Ibid. p. 15.

52: "There was no script for the agents' confrontation": Ibid., p. 25.

52: "The agents were just not part of the team": Harris phone interview, September 16, 2012.

53: "Offering Lewinsky a 'cooperation made known'": OSC report, p. 25.

53: "No one seems to have taken any steps at this time to try to determine whether this was a proper means of discouraging her from contacting Carter": Harris phone interview, June 26, 2014.

53: "There are two ways that the independent counsel can expand the jurisdiction": Ibid.

53: "It was important to be covered with 'belt and suspenders' for sensitive matters": OSC report, p. 18, footnote 11.

54: "Tripp's comment to Lewinsky that 'you didn't even tell your own attorney the truth': Ibid., p. 28, footnote 26.

54: "Tripp had arranged to meet Lewinsky": Ibid., p. 29.

55: "kids playing a game of 'T-Ball.'": Jo Ann Harris and Mary Francis Harkenrider, "Memorandum of Interview," Steve Irons, March 17, 2000, p. 2.

55: "Going to advise her of her rights": OSC report, p.30.

56: "This was OIC's investigation": Ibid., p. 33.

56: "Be especially careful not to cross the ethical line": Ibid., p. 34.

56: "We had to wing it . . . [he] had the tape [of her conversation with Tripp] cued-up and was prepared to play it for Lewinsky": Ibid., p. 34.

56: "As the day played out, she was apparently never confronted with the evidence against her": "Memorandum of Interview," FBI Special Agent Steve Irons, March 17, 2000, p. 4.

56: "This is not about Paula Jones": "Memorandum of Interview," FBI Special Agent Steve Irons, March 17, 2000, p. 4.

57: "free to leave": Jo Ann Harris and Mary Francis Harkenrider, "Memorandum of Interview," Monica Lewinsky, June 5, 2000, p. 3.

57: "The written record of what occurred": OSC report, p. 36.

57: "Why don't you hear us out": "Memorandum of Interview," Monica Lewinsky, June 5, 2000, p. 7.

58: "Emmick's conclusion 'that pre-indictment contact was always allowed, was simply wrong'": OSC report, p. 3.

58: "'Wine and cheese' approach": Jo Ann Harris and Mary Francis Harkenrider, "Memorandum of Interview," Patrick Fallon, May 4, 2000, p. 3.

58: "'Completely freaked out'": "Memorandum of Interview," Monica Lewinsky, June 5, 2000, p. 3.

58: "They were not concerned so much about Carter's complicity in the crime": Harris phone interview, September 16, 2012.

59: "'Lewinsky suggested taking a taxi to her attorney's office'": OSC report, p. 41.

59: "the civil and criminal cases were separate": Ibid., p. 42, footnote 55.

59: "It's one thing not to analyze a very complicated department policy": Harris phone interview, June 26, 2014.

60: "That tough little lady never folded": Harris phone interview, September 16, 2012.

60: "(*US v. Weiss*, 599 F. 2d at 741)": OSC report, p. 67.

Case citation: https://casetext.com/case/united-states-v-weiss-3

60: "You don't need to call your mommy": "Memorandum of Interview," Monica Lewinsky, June 5, 2000, p. 9.

61: "Lewinsky said that she was afraid she was being followed": OSC report, p. 45, footnote 62.

61: "Did they ever tell you that you could not call Mr. Carter": Juror, *Part 1, Appendices to the Referral to the United States House of Representatives Pursuant to Title 28, United States Code, § Section 595(c).*

Submitted by the Office of Independent Counsel, September 9, 1998, Tab 3, Grand Jury Proceedings, Monica S. Lewinsky, August 20, 1998, p. 1150.

Chapter 7

63: "Is there any truth to the allegation of an affair": Robert Siegel and Mara Liasson interview of Clinton, *All Things Considered,* National Public Radio, January 21, 1998.

63: "When the entire Monica Lewinsky thing hit": Merletti interview, November 7, 2007.

65: "Dear Agent Merletti": Monica Lewinsky letter to Lewis Merletti, October 28, 1996, Merletti files.

65: "When I brought the letter in": Merletti interview, November 7, 2007.

66: "Lewinsky saw a USSS plainclothes agent named Lou Merletti": *Part 1, Appendices to the Referral to the United States House of Representatives Pursuant to Title 28, United States Code, § Section 595(c). Submitted by the Office of Independent Counsel, September 9, 1998,* Tab 20, Continuation of FBI-302 of Monica Lewinsky on 07/30/98, p. 1430.

66: "When I made the very first presentation to Starr": Merletti interview, November 7, 2007.

67: "I call in the four, former living directors of the Secret Service": Ibid.

68: "They said, 'You have an hour and a half to make your case'": Ibid.

68: "The level of protection provided the president of the United States": Merletti speech: "National Academy (FBI) 'Leadership,' conference," March 30, 2000, pp. 3,10,11. Merletti files.

69: "President Andrew Jackson, January 30, 1835. No security present": Ibid.

70: "Four days *before* Dallas": Merletti interview, November 7, 2007.

73: "'I hoped that this picture would never come out'": Ibid.

74: "'We failed our mission. The president died, and it was *my* fault'": Ibid.

74: "'And, I will be by your side at every court appearance'": Merletti phone interview, July 1, 2015.

75: "Was there anything that the Secret Service or that Clint Hill could have done": Mike Wallace, *60 Minutes*, December 7, 1975.

76: "Very powerful, very convincing; *very, very* powerful": Merletti interview, November 7, 2007.

76: "We find it hard to believe that he couldn't see this": Ibid.

76-77: "In a detailed, twelve-page timeline": Misha Travers memo, "Subject: Secret Service timeline," Records of Independent Counsel Kenneth W. Starr/Robert Ray/Julie Thomas files, National Archives and Records Administration, July 2, 1998.

77: "This office has great respect for the work you and your agents do": Merletti interview, November 7, 2007.

77: "Reno could only intervene for good cause": 28 USC Ch. 40: Independent Counsel; Statutory Notes and Related Subsidiaries; §596. Removal of an independent counsel, https://uscode.house.gov/view. xhtml?path=/prelim@title28/part2/chapter40&edition=prelim

77: "Merletti received numerous unsolicited messages from law enforcement agencies": (1) Email, To Merletti, From [redacted], Denver, CO, January 27, 1998; (2) Email, To Merletti, From [redacted], Skokie, IL, January 28, 1998; (3) Email, To Merletti, From [redacted],

Birmingham, AL, January 28, 1998; (4) Email, To Merletti, From [redacted], Seattle, WA, January 28, 1998; (5) Email, To Merletti, From [redacted], Richmond, VA, January 29, 1998; (6) Email, To Merletti, From [redacted], Kent, WA, January 29, 1998; (7) Email, To Merletti, From [redacted], La Jolla, CA, January 29, 1998; (8) Email, To Merletti, From [redacted], Highland MI, January 30, 1998; (9) Press Release, Fraternal Order of Police, District of Columbia, January 30, 1998; (10) Letter, Office of the Attorney General, Tallahassee, Florida, April 16, 1998; (11) Email, [outside organization], To Merletti, From [redacted] May 19, 1998; (12) Email, To Merletti, From [redacted], May 26, 1998; (13) Email, USSS To the Director, From [Redacted], June 4, 1998; (14) Email, To Merletti, From [redacted], June 4, 1998; (15) Email, To Merletti, From [redacted], June 9, 1998, Merletti files.

78: The Department of Justice "has agreed to provide you with legal representation in your official capacity'": Deputy Assistant Attorney General Gary Grindler letter addressed to Lewis C. Merletti, March 19, 1998, Merletti files,

78: "'This isn't right,' Bush told him in a phone call": Merletti interview, November 7, 2007.

79: "Well, my view differs": President George H. W. Bush, speech before Harvard Kennedy School, May 28, 1998.

79: "Dear Lew": Personal letter from President George H.W. Bush to Lewis Merletti, April 15, 1998, Merletti files.

Chapter 8

81: "We find that neither the regulation, its commentary, nor other department materials provide a clear and unambiguous answer to [the] question [of whether Lewinsky was represented by Carter]": Office of

Special Counsel Report, Office of Special Counsel (OSC) files within the Starr, Ray, Thomas, Office of Independent Counsel (OIC) files, National Archives and Records Administration (NARA), p. 70-71.

82: "It didn't make any difference if Mike had advocated caution": Bruce Udolf phone interview, July 24, 2019.

82: "We have found poor judgment in overall stewardship of the confrontation with Lewinsky": OSC report, p. 88.

83: "I thought it was the fair thing to do": Harris phone interview, June 2014.

83: "I was distraught": Michael Emmick phone conversation, contemporaneous, handwritten note (opposite page 24 of OSC report), based on his last email, November 3, 2014.

83: "Michael Emmick is 'a dedicated, talented public servant who, in this one instance, simply did not exercise the good judgment expected of federal prosecutors'": OSC report, p. 8.

84: "the two recommended 'that you reject the report's finding'": "Office of Independent Counsel, Memorandum to Robert W. Ray, from J. Keith Ausbrook, Julie F. Thomas, January 16, 2001," OIC files.

84: "You guys want to trade on our statements'": "OSC issues with the OIC's Rendition of OSC's Summary." Undated memo faxed from Jo Ann Harris to Keith Ausbrook, Office of Independent Counsel, OSC/OIC files.

84: "For months, Harris and Ray traded summaries": February 1 to sometime in May 2001. Chronology compiled by the author from a phone conversation, July 29, 2014, vetted by Harris.

85: "Ray abbreviated special counsels' one-hundred-page report and his rebuttal into two and a quarter-pages": Robert W. Ray, *Final Report of the Independent Counsel: In Re: Madison Guaranty Savings*

& Loan Association Regarding Monica Lewinsky and Others, March 6, 2002, pp. 106-108.

85: "Harris, angered, submitted rebuttal comments to the court attaching an 'exhibit' (a copy of her report)": Harris letter addressed to the Honorable Mark J. Langer, Clerk, Special Division, January 9, 2002, OSC/OIC files.

85: "In a second letter to the court": Harris's addressed to the Honorable Mark J. Langer, Clerk Special Division, February 16, 2002, OSC/OIC files.

86: "'Both Ms. Harkenrider and I believe it is important to our professional reputations'": Harris's third letter addressed to The Honorable Judges of the Special Division, February 18, 2002. OSC/OIC files.

86: "Judge Garland is recused in the matter": Response letter from Tracy Hauser Scarrow, special assistant to Chief Judge Merrick Garland, August 19, 2014.

86: "The Special Division no longer exists": Response letter from Judge David B. Sentelle, September 5, 2014.

86: "*Outrageous*": special counsel Jo Ann Harris's reaction to Sentelle letter, phone conversation, contemporaneous notes, September 16, 2014.

87: "He explained that his attorney obtained a court order sealing Harris's report and would have her provide me with a copy of the order": Email from Michael Emmick, September 22, 2014.

87: "If the special counsel report prepared by Jo Ann Harris": Email from Robert Reed, September 17, 2014, NARA.

88: "I asked Harris who at OIC had told her that her report was sealed": Harris phone conversation, contemporaneous notes, September 16, 2014.

88: "Is this going to be window dressing": Phone interview with Mary Harkenrider, contemporaneous notes, October 23, 2014.

88: "William Barr, then attorney general, mischaracterized special counsel Robert Mueller's summary": David A. Graham, "Barr Misled the Public—and It Worked," *The Atlantic*, May 1, 2019, https://www.theatlantic.com/ideas/archive/2019/05/barr-misled-the-publicand-it-worked/588463/.

89: "'The Special Counsel's investigation revealed that there were many others involved'": Robert W. Ray, *Final Report of the Independent Counsel: In Re: Madison Guaranty Savings & Loan Association Regarding Monica Lewinsky and Others, March 6, 2002*, p. 108.

89-90: "'Hochberg suggested that if OIC had concerns about Carter's reliability . . . Hochberg also raised DOJ's regulation regarding contacting a person who has a lawyer.'": OSC report, p. 22.

90: "'Most of OIC's lawyers with whom we talked, including Emmick'": Ibid., p. 24.

90-91: "'Every independent counsel office should appoint a PRO [professional responsibility officer]'": Jo Ann Harris abbreviates OSC's recommendations in a phone conversation, OSC report, pp. 99-100.

Chapter 9

94: "OPR is typically black and white about matters": Robert Bittman phone interview, August 22, 2014.

94: "Bittman said it was called 'the deliberative process'": Jo Ann Harris and Mary Francis Harkenrider, "Memorandum of Interview,"

Robert J. Bittman, June 27, 2000, Office of Special Counsel (OSC), Office of Independent Counsel (OIC) files, The National Archives and Records Administration (NARA), p. 1.

94: "'The process' according to Wisenberg, is an inside joke": Jo Ann Harris and Mary Francis Harkenrider, "Memorandum of Interview," Solomon L. Wisenberg, May 15, 2000, OSC/OIC files, NARA, p. 3.

94: "Rather at meetings, often someone would suggest pulling out DOJ regs on relevant issues": Harris and Harkenrider, "Memorandum of Interview," Robert J. Bittman, p. 1.

94: "Sam Dash . . . 'cleared us on approach night'": Harris and Harkenrider, "Memorandum of Interview," Solomon L. Wisenberg, p. 4, footnote 5.

95: "Wisenberg regarded the Lewinsky matter as 'the case of the century'": Ibid., p. 3.

95-96: "We consulted with him occasionally": Solomon Wisenberg phone interview, October 15, 2018.

101: "All OIC lawyers involved had the obligation to ensure that they were proceeding ethically": OSC report, p. 15.

101 "The Department of Justice made a strong commitment to enforce vigorously the contacts rules": OSC report, p. 5.

103: "Smart-alecky Beverly Hills know-it-all": Bates's notes "Monica meeting 1/17/98," (internal OIC document p. 16). NARA I.D.: 15770 DocId: 70102080, p. 29.

103: "'Where do you get off offering immunity . . .' Bennett demanded": Harris and Harkenrider, "Memorandum of Interview," Solomon L. Wisenberg, p. 4.

104: "Sam Dash . . . 'outside independent expert'": Jo Ann Harris and Mary Francis Harkenrider, "Memorandum of Interview" of Sam Dash, May 16, 2000, OSC/OIC files, p. 1.

105: "'I was really surprised to hear that he wasn't consulted,' Harris told me": Jo Ann Harris interview, September 16, 2012.

105: "'I saw decisions made on moral grounds'": Sidney Blumenthal, *The Clinton Wars*, New York: Farrar, Straus and Giroux, 2003), p. 382.

105: "'One of Starr's problems'": Ibid. pp. 385-386.

106: "he threatened to quit on more than one occasion . . . [and] said he knew nothing about the Tripp and Lewinsky matter until he read about it in the paper": Jo Ann Harris and Mary Francis Harkenrider, "Memorandum of Interview," Sam Dash, p. 1.

106: "What do you mean? We called her lawyer": Harris and Harkenrider, "Memorandum of Interview," Sam Dash, p. 1.

106: If a caller needed to contact Carter, his answering service had three ways to reach him. "Memorandum of Interview," Frank Carter, June 6, 2000, p. 1

107: "a dumb strategy": "Memorandum of Interview," Sam Dash, p. 2, footnote 2.

107: "Dash stated that if he thought 'they sought to dissuade her from representation,' he would have been very troubled": Ibid., p. 2.

108: "Starr stated that the office had a designated ethics officer to deal with the Government Ethics Act": Harris and Harkenrider, "Memorandum of Interview," Kenneth W. Starr, June 23-24, 2000, OSC/OIC files, p. 2.

108: "applicable DOJ policy on any specific issue": Ethics are part of DOJ policies as described on the Department of Justice website, listed under "Standards of Conduct," https://www.justice.gov/jm/jm-1-4000-standards-conduct#1-4.100

Chapter 10

109: "Tripp/Lewinsky tapes and in Tripp's statements": Office of Special Counsel Report, Office of Special Counsel (OSC) files within the Starr, Ray, Thomas Office of Independent Counsel (OIC) files, National Archives and Records Administration (NARA), p. 19, footnote 12.

110: "David Margolis . . . could be approached to review the facts in sensitive cases": OSC report, p. 23, footnote 17.

110: "[OIC's] good faith could never have been questioned afterward": Ibid., p. 89, footnote 115.

112: "The way in which Lewinsky ended up with Carter": Ibid., p. 19, footnote 12.

112: "General overconfidence in his own expertise": Ibid., p. 98.

113: "I regret a great deal": Michael Emmick phone interview, contemporaneous notes taken, November 3, 2014.

113: "The world is often much more complex": Email from Emmick, November 3, 2014.

113: "I may not be here in a couple of days": Harris cell phone conversation, contemporaneous notes, October 2014.

114: "I don't think we ought to be investigating crap like this": Harris phone interview, September 16, 2012.

114: "I think they, [the Special Division], took the only professional prosecutor": Ibid.

115: "'Keep Fiske'": Harris phone interview, Ibid.

David Johnston, "Reno Wants to Reappoint Fiske under New Law," *The New York Times*, July 2, 1994, https://www.nytimes.com/1994/07/02/us/reno-wants-to-reappoint-fiske-under-a-new-law.html.

115: "Seven months into his investigation, the reasoning used in replacing Fiske": "Timeline for Watergate Investigation," *The Washington Post,* https://www.washingtonpost.com/wp-srv/politics/special/whitewater/timeline.htm. (Fiske was appointed in January 1994 and replaced August 5, 1994.)

115: "Fiske's sweeping investigative focus": Ken Starr, *Contempt: A Memoir of the Clinton Investigation,* (New York: Sentinel, 2018), p. 50.

Chapter 11

117: "We dress as soldiers, doctors, engineers, graduates": Merletti interview, November 7, 2007.

118-119: "This letter is addressed to Senator Kerry": Letter from secret service director John Magaw to Senator John F. Kerry, July 24, 1992, Merletti files.

120-21: "We go in, big conference room, me and Kelleher": Merletti interview, November 7, 2007.

122: "We're going to fight and fight and *fight!*": Ibid.

122: "Waxman was unable to recall any additional information": Response letter from former Solicitor General Seth P. Waxman, March 25, 2013.

122-123: "Senate Judiciary Committee for a yet-to-be-numbered Senate bill": August 13, 1998, Senate Bill, Merletti files.

Chapter 12

125: "You wrote several praising things about Merletti": Robert Bittman phone interview, August 22, 2014.

127-128: "In a 'Talking Points' memo prepared for a March 29, 1998 meeting": "Talking Points for 3/29/98 on 'Protective Function' privilege," Robert Bittman attorney work files, Office of Independent Counsel (OIC) files, National Archives and Records Administration (NARA), p. 1, points 1 - 6.

127: "at least be subject to the exception recognized in *US v. Nixon*": Ibid., point 3.

Case citation: *United States vs. Nixon*, 418 US 683 (1974); Justia US Supreme Court. The primary holding states: "The President cannot shield himself from producing evidence in a criminal prosecution based on the doctrine of executive privilege, although it is valid in other situations": https://supreme.justia.com/cases/federal/us/418/683/

128: "under no circumstances are any tapes monitored": United States Government Memorandum, US Secret Service, "To: Inspector Dagg; From: SAIC Sims; Subject: Secret Service Participation in Taping," The Miller Center, December 6, 1973, p. 4.

128: "it never happened to my knowledge": Email from Louis Sims; August 31, 2021.

128: "The claim that the privilege extends to hearsay": "Talking Points for 3/29/98 on 'Protective Function' privilege," Robert Bittman attorney work files, OIC files, point 6.

128: "Even if OIC recognized the privilege": Robert Bittman phone interview, August 22, 2014.

129: "If a Secret Service agent saw RN [Richard Nixon] burning the tapes": Kenneth Starr personal notes (notepad), April 1998, p. 25, OIC files.

131: "'We have bent over backwards'": Letter from Jackie Bennett to Eric Holder, April 17, 1998, OIC files.

132: "'The people who handled this on the part of DOJ were obstructionists'": Robert Bittman phone interview, August 22, 2014.

133: "Someone at that meeting said, 'We have information that *you*, Mr. Merletti'": Lewis Merletti interview, November 7, 2007.

133: "[OIC] gave up when their informant, whom they assured of confidentiality, refused to go on the record": Susan Schmidt and Michael Weisskopf, *Truth at Any Cost,* p. 137.

133: "Several things about tips": Robert Bittman phone interview, August 22, 2014.

134: "a lot of nut calls": Solomon Wisenberg phone interview, October 15, 2018.

135: "'We have specific and credible information'": "Talking Points for 3/29/98 Meeting on 'Protective Function' privilege," Robert Bittman attorney work files, p. 1, point 9.

135: "'I don't want to hear anything coming from any Secret Service agents about girls'": Office of Independent Counsel Memo, From Jackie M. Bennett, Jr., Subject: Telephone call re: Secret Service privilege issue, March 2, 1998, OIC files.

136: "'That would be a negative,' Kelleher said": John Keller phone conversation, contemporaneous notes cited in author's email to Kat Mathis, December 29, 2014.

137: "In January, Paula Jones's lawyers had tried to subpoena four Secret Service agents": *The Death of American Virtue,* by Ken Gormley, (Crown Publishers, 2010), p. 487.

Chapter 13

139: "denying a stay": "Text of Chief Justice Rehnquist's Order Denying Secret Service Stay": CNN, https://www.cnn. com/ALLPOLITICS/1998/07/17/lewinsky/order.html   [Accessed: 09/21/2021].

139: "Cockell wasn't even *on* PPD": personal notes re: Ken Starr, Merletti files.

140: "'Wait a minute,' FBI Director Louis Freeh told Starr": Louis J. Freeh with Howard Means, *My FBI, Bringing Down the MAFIA, Investigating Bill Clinton, and Fighting the War on Terror,* (New York: St. Martin's Press, 2005), p. 265.

140: "the Marine Corps Law Enforcement Foundation": Merletti interview, November 7, 2007.

141: "FBI lab work": Ken Starr personal notes (notepad), July 1998, p. 8, Office of Independent Counsel (OIC) files, National Archives and Records Administration (NARA).

141: "Tom Pickard": Ken Starr personal notes (notepad), March 1998, Ibid., p. 13.

141: "An individual who had not only worked for MCLEF but was the co-chair of the event in 1998": Conversation with former co-chair (Mike) at MCLEF, February 19, 2015.

142: "I *did* have a conversation with Clinton": Merletti phone conversation, December 29, 2014.

142: "The reason I retired": Ron Williams, "A Secret Service Agent Who Guarded Clinton Speaks Up," *Orange County Register* Opinion, October 31, 1996, Merletti files.

143: "You can't hide this thing": Merletti phone interview, December 29, 2014.

143: "I am compelled to write": USSS Director Eljay B. Bowron, "Ex-Agent Speaks for Himself," *Orange County Register* Opinion, November 4, 1996, Merletti files.

144: "I want to apologize": Letter addressed to USSS Director Eljay Bowron, November 8, 1996, Merletti files.

144: "He interviewed these four Secret Service guys": Merletti interview, November 7, 2007.

144: "one agent Hersh interviewed gave long and detailed narratives of the president's habits": derived from Seymour M. Hersh, *The Dark Side of Camelot*, (New York: Little Brown, 1997).

145: "We came forward about Kennedy": Merletti phone interview, December 29, 2014.

145: "Four former Secret Service agents are quoted": Director Merletti memo, "Subject: 'The Dark Side of Camelot,'" December 5, 1997, Merletti files.

145: "'You knew we were coming'": Merletti interview, November 7, 2007.

145: "That might have been before Lewinsky": Solomon Wisenberg phone interview, October 15, 2018.

146: "Safeguarding Communications": Memo from USSS Director Eljay Bowron, March 26, 1996, Merletti files.

146: "Inaccurate, unsubstantiated rumors about the service": Memo from USSS Director John Magaw to *Newsweek* magazine president/editor-in-chief Richard Smith, August 20, 1993, Merletti files.

148: "Memorandum for Secretary Norton; Protection of the President," June 8, 1910, Merletti files.

148: "It's not just my idea. It's *everyone's* idea": Merletti interview, November 7, 2007.

149: "Direct Observations of the President and Monica Lewinsky in a Compromising Position": OIC memo from Mischa Travers, "Subject: Secret Service, Some Parting Thoughts," July 6, 1998, p. 6, OIC files.

149: "'Very upset. Hysterical,' she told the grand jury": *Part 1, Appendices to the Referral to the United States House of Representatives Pursuant to Title 28, United States Code, Section § 595(c) Submitted by the Office of Independent Counsel, September 9, 1998*, Tab 2, Grand Jury proceedings, p. 831.

150: "[Agent] has following PFP observations/communications": OIC memo from Mischa Travers, "Subject: Secret Service, Some Parting Thoughts," July 6, 1998, p. 9.

150: "*The Dallas Morning News* reported that a current or former Secret Service agent claimed to have witnessed Clinton and Lewinsky in an 'ambiguous incident.' Hours later, the paper retracted the story'": Howard Kurtz, "Dallas Paper's Story Traveled Far Before Being Shot Down," *The Washington Post*, January 28, 1998, https://www.washingtonpost.com/archive/lifestyle/1998/01/28/dallas-papers-story-traveled-far-before-being-shot-down/5818f7cd-0baa-459f-a33d-5d5d07380516/

150: "New York tabloid carried the headline: 'Secret Service agent to testify: I SAW THEM DO IT'": *The New York Post*, January 27, 1998.

151: "There are other doors in and out [of the Oval Office]": Merletti interview, November 7, 2007.

151: "purposely departed by a different door than the one she had entered, so that the USSS staff would not know when Lewinsky came and left": Monica Lewinsky's Third Interview, Office of the Independent Counsel, July 30, 1998; *Part 1, Appendices to the Referral to the United States House of Representatives Pursuant to Title 28, United States Code, § Section 595(c). Submitted by the Office of Independent Counsel,* September 9, 1998, Tab 20, interview of Monica Lewinsky, 07/30/98, p. 1436.

151: "We came to learn": personal notes, Merletti files.

151: "Starr 'assigned scores of FBI agents,' Merletti notated": personal notes re: Ken Starr, 2, Merletti files.

151: "This is Carl Rowan": "Common Sense and the Secret Service," Carl Rowen, *The Buffalo News*, teletype, May 28, 1998.

152: "Starr Mistook His Job as Hunt for the Truth Instead of Justice": Larry Eichel, *The Philadelphia Inquirer*, May 2, 1998, (Link unavailable; scanned from newsprint.)

152: "Shaped by a Painful Past, Secret Service Director Fights Required Testimony": John M Broder, and Stephen Labaton, *The New York Times*, May 30, 1998, https://www.nytimes.com/1998/05/30/us/shaped-by-a-painful-past-secret-service-director-fights-required-testimony.html

152: "Secret Service Privilege: A Matter of Life or Death": Albert R. Hunt, *The Wall Street Journal*, June 4, 1998, https://www.wsj.com/articles/SB896913306270291500

152: "Assassination Risk Cited in Ex-Agents' Brief to Block Queries": Peter Baker, *The Washington Post*, June 16, 1998, https://

www.washingtonpost.com/wp-srv/politics/special/clinton/stories/service061698.htm

Brief: *In the United States Court of Appeals for the District of Columbia Circuit, In Re: Grand Jury Proceedings; On Appeal from the United States District Court for the District of Columbia; Brief for Amici Curiae in Support of the United States Secret Service Filed with Consent of the Parties*, June 26, 1998, Merletti files.

152: "'I was against having agents testify,' McCarthy said": Philip H. Melanson, Ph. D; "The Secret Service: The Hidden History of an Enigmatic Agency," (New York: Basic Books 2005), p. 310.

152: "Chris Von Holt, another agent brought before Ken Starr's grand jury": Ibid.

153: "Robert L. DeProspero, who headed Reagan's security detail": "Starr vs. Secret Service: Two Definitions of Duty," Peter Baker, *The Washington Post*, May 15, 1998, https://www.washingtonpost.com/archive/politics/1998/05/15/starr-vs-secret-service-two-definitions-of-duty/695577fc-5c92-4c53-92b5-76e554c0f6fc/

153: "'If you don't have trust and confidence, you don't have proximity,' said Edward P. Walsh": Ibid.

153: "'That's nonsense,' former Kennedy agent Tony Sherman told investigative reporter Seymour Hersh": Ibid.

153: "Compelling testimony from those entrusted with the security of the President": quote by Theodore C. Sorensen, "When the Secret Service Talks," *The New York Times Opinion*, July 19, 1998, https://www.nytimes.com/1998/07/19/opinion/when-the-secret-service-talks.html

154: "In essence, the courts have held": quote by Laurence Tribe: Ibid.

154: "Look at this here": Merletti referencing diagram of West Wing offices. "Grand Jury Tries to Determine Lines of Sight," Dan Balz, *The Washington Post*, February 6, 1998.

Merletti referencing a second diagram of West Wing offices, "White House No Magic Carpet Ride," Mimi Hall, *USA Today*, February 5, 1998. Merletti interview, November 7, 2007.

155: "I had received probably dozens [of media requests]": Merletti interview, November 7, 2007.

155: "In 1901, we're protecting [President] McKinley": Merletti takes the author through a paper printout of an edited PowerPoint presentation given to Independent Counsel Ken Starr, Deputy Robert Bittman; Department of Justice officials including US deputy attorney general Eric Holder, and US attorney general Janet Reno, Merletti interview, November 7, 2007, and his speech to the "National Academy (FBI) "Leadership," March 30, 2000, pp. 3, 4, 6, 7, 8, 9, 12, Merletti files.

Chapter 14

159: "Jim, Folder 23 also has a June 6, 1998 letter (signed 'Deep Throat')": Email from Robert Reed, National Archives and Records Administration, (NARA), July 16, 2015.

160: "The first page is a copy of a letter" and "Association of Former Agents of the US Secret Service, Inc.": Email from Robert Reed, (NARA), July 17, 2015.

160: "The second page appears to be drafted by someone": Unsigned memo dated January 29, 1998, Ibid.

161-162: "Dear Judge Starr": "Deep Throat" letter addressed to Ken Starr, June 6, 1998, Ibid.

162: "The number matched one of two fax lines at the Centerville Drive address in Little Rock": Telephone List, January 8, 1998. Record Group 449: Records of Independent Counsel Kenneth W. Starr, W. Hickman Ewing Attorney Work Files, Chronological File, January 1998 Washington, DC manifest, (DC Box 1707).

162: "W. Hickman Ewing, Jr. . . . developed a taste for prosecuting political corruption":

"Some Say Dad's Travails Led Hickman Ewing to Law Center," Glenn R. Simpson, *The Wall Street Journal*, July 31, 1996, https://www.wsj.com/articles/SB838765616306277000

163: "Astonishing recall—of Hickman Ewing": Ken Starr, *Contempt: A Memoir of the Clinton Investigation,* (New York: Sentinel, 2019), p. 313.

164: "I feel like I've been victimized all over again": Merletti phone conversation, July 17, 2015.

164: "Unfortunately, no": Email response from Rodger Heaton, May 14, 2016.

164: "I am sorry, but I really don't have a direct memory of this": Email response from Paul Rosenzweig, July 18, 2015.

164: "I never met the tipster": Email response from Paul Rosenzweig, May 15, 2016.

165: "I really can't. I knew we got tips at various times": Solomon Wisenberg phone interview, October 15, 2018.

166: "Why is this so important? We got lots of tips": Solomon Wisenberg phone conversation, contemporaneous notes, July 18, 2015.

166: "The case of the century": Harris and Harkenrider, "Memorandum of Interview," Solomon L. Wisenberg, May 15, 2000, Office of Special Counsel (OSC), Office of Independent Counsel (OIC) files within the Starr, Ray, Thomas Office of Independent Counsel files, National Archives and Records Administration (NARA).

166: "The head of each Federal agency shall make and preserve records": The Federal Records Act; § 3101. Records management by agency heads; general duties, https://www.archives.gov/about/laws/fed-agencies.html

166: [including those] received by an agency of the United States Government": What is a Record?; https://www.archives.gov/records-mgmt/faqs/federal.html

167: "'Copies of the same document filed in multiple attorney files'": Email response from Robert Reed, NARA, December 15, 2020.

167: "I'm not certain that Ewing's journal is a federal record.": Email from Robert Reed, NARA, June 17, 2023.

Chapter 15

169: "Good evening. This afternoon in this room": Clinton public apology statement, August 17, 1998.

169: [Kelleher], "It's over, Lew": Merletti interview, November 7, 2007.

170: "Director, Ken Starr. Well, it's over": Ibid.

170: "I had never met anyone with such an attitude of superiority": personal notes, p. 2, Merletti files.

170: "We are going by the book. We want the truth": Public Broadcasting Service (PBS) interview of Ken Starr, February 5, 1998.

170: "Well, I really think Starr was over his head": Harris phone interview, June 26, 2014.

171: "Judiciary Panel Signals It Will Pursue Impeachment," Ruth Marcus, *The Washington Post*, November 10, 1998, https://www.

washingtonpost.com/archive/politics/1998/11/10/judiciary-panel-signals-it-will-pursue-impeachment/6b77df37-9d05-4327-9d97-5b9d398b71c9/

171: "Secret Service Director Retiring to Work for Pro Football Team," John M. Broder, *The New York Times*, November 13, 1998.

Chapter 16

173: "I just got a call from the FBI": Merletti interview, November 7, 2007.

174: "On January 18, 2001, Merletti arrived in Washington expecting to face a grand jury": "Subpoena to Testify before Grand Jury," January 18, 2001, Merletti files.

174: "You're the last person who can give us the information": Merletti interview, November 7, 2007.

175: "In all 18 interviews, 2 grand jury appearances, and a deposition": *Part 1, Appendices to the Referral to the United States House of Representatives Pursuant to Title 28, United States Code, Section § 595(c). Submitted by the Office of Independent Counsel, September 9, 1998*; Tabs 18-35, pp. 1389-1603.

175: "'not attempt to protect any person or entity through false information or omission'": *Part 1, Appendices to the Referral to the United States House of Representatives Pursuant to Title 28, United States Code, Section § 595(c). Submitted by the Office of Independent Counsel, September 9, 1998*, Tab K, Monica Lewinsky Immunity Agreement, pp. 378-379.

175: "And no such line of questioning about Merletti's involvement took place during President Clinton's grand jury testimony, as well": "President Clinton's grand jury testimony": *Part 1, Appendices to the*

Referral to the United States House of Representatives Pursuant to Title 28, United States Code, Section § 595(c). Submitted by the Office of Independent Counsel, September 9, 1998, William Jefferson Clinton, Tab 16, pp. 453–628.

175: "'OK, hold it,' Merletti told Gant": Merletti interview, November 7, 2007.

176: "I'm not in a position to comment": Judge Monte Richardson, contemporaneous notes from a phone interview, January 6, 2015.

177: "I don't recall seeing any confidentiality agreements": Email from Robert Reed, National Archives and Records Administration (NARA), May 30, 2019.

177: "Notes of the session, maintained by a source who wished to remain anonymous": Ken Gormley, *The Death of American Virtue: Clinton vs. Starr*, (New York: Crown Publishers, 2010), p. 758.

178: "'The reason for the meeting,' the source said": anonymous source, phone interview, December 3, 2014.

179: "Merletti told me, confirming this with a copy of business cards from everyone in attendance": copy of business cards, Merletti files.

Chapter 17

185: "By a 'committee of the whole'": Harris and Harkenrider, "Memorandum of Interview" of Kenneth W. Starr, June 23, and June 24, 2000, Office of Special Counsel (OSC) files within the Starr, Ray, Thomas Office of Independent Counsel (OIC) files, The National Archives and Records Administration (NARA), p. 1.

185: Wisenberg "described it as 'flat, open'": Harris and Harkenrider, "Memorandum of Interview" of Solomon L. Wisenberg, May 15, 2000, OSC/OIC files, NARA, p. 1.

185: "Bruce Udolf characterized OIC as working like a 'law school study group'": Harris and Harkenrider, "Memorandum of Interview," Bruce Udolf, April 3, 2000, OSC/OIC files, p. 2.

185: "Emmick described the decision-making process as 'terribly unwieldy'": Harris and Harkenrider, "Memorandum of Interview," Michael Emmick, April 4, 2000, OSC/OIC files, p. 2.

186: "'If it turns out we need to offer complete immunity'": Ibid., p. 6.

186: "Starr stated he did not recall any further meeting before the attorneys left for the Ritz": Harris and Harkenrider, "Memorandum of Interview," Kenneth W. Starr, OSC/OIC files p. 4.

186: "Starr . . . stated that at the time they thought Lewinsky's attorney was complicit": Ibid., p. 2.

186: "Starr 'did not recall' thirteen times concerning details of two critical meetings": Ibid., p. 4.

187: "Starr 'does not recall' . . . fifteen times": Harris and Harkenrider, "Memorandum of Interview," Kenneth W. Starr.

187: "Jackie Bennett . . . ten times": Harris and Harkenrider, "Memorandum of Interview," Jackie Bennett, June 22, 2000, OSC/OIC files.

187: "Robert Bittman, nine": Harris and Harkenrider, "Memorandum of Interview," Robert J. Bittman, June 27, 2000, OSC/OIC files.

187: "Solomon Wisenberg, two": Harris and Harkenrider, "Memorandum of Interview," Solomon L. Wisenberg, May 15, 2000.

187: "Sam Dash, none": Harris and Harkenrider, "Memorandum of Interview," Samuel Dash, May 16, 2000, OSC/OIC files.

187: "Josh Hochberg, none": Jo Ann Harris and Mary Francis Harkenrider, "Memorandum of Interview," Josh Hochberg, March 16, 2000, OSC/OIC files.

187: "[Starr] does not recall . . . the specifics of a briefing" and "precise statements": "Memorandum of Interview" of Kenneth W. Starr, pp. 3–4.

187: "Deliberative process," "collegial nonhierarchical structure": Ibid., p. 1.

187: "The job of the Deputies": Ibid., p. 2.

187: "Prosecution memos," "teams of lawyers assigned to various matters": Ibid., p. 1.

187: "Cited the Denton matter": Ibid., p. 2.

187: "Detailed the chronology of his involvement in the Lewinsky matter": Ibid., p. 3.

187: "Starr . . . did not recall any statement regarding a *Margolis* procedure": Ibid., p. 4.

187-188: "Hochberg vividly recalls": Harris and Harkenrider, "Memorandum of Interview," Josh Hochberg, p. 2.

188: "Margolis 'was regarded . . . as an all-knowing Yoda-like figure'": Eric Lichtblau, "David Margolis, A Justice Department Institution, Dies 76," *The New York Times*, July 15, 2016, https://www.nytimes.com/2016/07/16/us/david-margolis-a-justice-Department-institution-dies-at-76.html

188: "Starr replied that Mike Emmick had looked at the issue": Harris and Harkenrider, "Memorandum of Interview," Josh Hochberg, p. 2.

188: "Hochberg recalls that he was still uncomfortable": Ibid., p. 3.

188: "Fifteen pages of notes": Ibid., pp. 5–22.

189: "Frank Keating": Ken Starr personal notes (notepad), April 22, 1998, OIC files, p. 25.

189: "This week—Frank Keating": Ibid.

189: "Had lunch with Frank Keating": Ken Starr personal notes (notepad), May 1998, p. 7.

189: "Agents should not be talking about purely private matters": Peter Baker, *The Washington Post*, May 15, 1998, https://www.washingtonpost.com/archive/politics/1998/05/15/starr-vs-secret-service-two-definitions-of-duty/695577fc-5c92-4c53-92b5-76e554c0f6fc/

190: "David Bossie, a Republican congressman hired by Dan Burton as chief investigator of Clinton": Wikipedia, [Access date: 12-27-2022] https://en.wikipedia.org/wiki/David_Bossie.

190-191: "Portrait of a Political 'Pit Bull,'": Russ Baker, *Salon*, December 22, 1998, https://www.salon.com/1998/12/22/newsa950556369/.

191: "Vince Foster . . . had been murdered": House speech, August 2, 1994; Eric Kleefeld, "Great Moments in Dan Burton History," *Talking Points Memo* (TPM), January 31, 2012, https://talkingpointsmemo.com/election2012/great-moments-in-dan-burton-history.

191: "A conspiracy theory that three investigations had disproved": Sean Wilentz, "Why Was Kavanaugh Obsessed with Vince Foster?" *The New York Times*, September 5, 2018.

"Fiske concluded in 1994"; "Official accounts by the National Park Service in 1993 and by a Republican congressman, William Clinger came to an identical conclusion," https://www.nytimes.com/2018/09/05/opinion/why-was-kavanaugh-obsessed-with-vince-foster.html.

191: "I just called to give you encouragement": Ken Starr personal notes (notepad), May 1998, p. 4.

192: "I would not have taken the job": Harris phone interview, September 16, 2012.

192: "Bob Points": Ken Starr personal notes (notepad), May 6, 1998, p. 10.

193: "Secret Service . . . Sam Dash . . . Mike Shaheen . . . Litigation team . . . Jackie . . . quality of source info": Ken Starr personal notes (notepad), March 1998, p. 97.

193: "perceived ethical lapses by the nation's highest officials": Dennis Hevesi, *The New York Times*, December 11, 2007, https://www.nytimes.com/2007/12/11/washington/11shaheen.html

193: "This would be a live grenade": Ken Starr personal notes (notepad), July 1998, p. 2.

193: "We need Monica or Secret Service": Ken Starr personal notes (notepad), July 1998, p. 9.

194: "Even an internal OIC memo documenting a timeline of the Secret Service matter lists the first meeting": Misha Travers memo, "Subject: Secret Service timeline," July 2, 1998, OIC files, p. 1.

195. "He was obsessed with public relations": *The Clinton Wars*, Sidney Blumenthal, (New York: Farrar, Straus and Giroux, 2003), p. 386.

196: "Frivolous. . . novel idea . . . bizarre notion . . . cleverly invented . . . heretical doctrine . . . cleverly invented": Ken Starr, *Contempt: A Memoir of the Clinton Investigation.* (New York: Sentinel, 2018), p. 214.

196: "Bogus": Ibid., p. 225.

196: "Ginned-up": Ibid., p. 248.

196: "The Solicitor General's Office helped": Ibid., p. 214.

197: "Judge Susan Webber Wright in *Jones v. Clinton*": "Memorandum for Attorney General Janet Reno. Subject: Testimonial Privilege for United States Secret Service Protective Function Personnel," February 17, 1998, p. 11, footnote 5, Merletti files.

198: "[Clinton] confided in no one and conspired with no one": Bob Woodward, *Shadow: Five Presidents and the Legacy of Watergate*, (New York: Simon & Schuster; 1999), p. 515.

198: "'Facts are stubborn things'": (Ken Starr quoting John Adams), Ken Starr, *Contempt: A Memoir of the Clinton Investigation*, (New York: Sentinel, 2018), p. 246.

198: "and whatever may be our wishes, our inclinations, or the dictates of our passion, they cannot alter the state of facts and evidence": John Adams, *Argument in Defense of the Soldiers in the Boston Massacre Trials*, December 1770, http://www.quotationspage.com/quote/3235. html

199-200: "I resign for a fundamental reason": Samuel Dash resignation letter, November 20, 1998; Robert W. Ray, *Final Report of the Independent Counsel: In Re: Madison Guaranty Savings & Loan Association; Regarding Monica Lewinsky and Others*, March 6, 2002, pp. 215 –216.

200: "Dash was not informed": Harris and Harkenrider, "Memorandum of Interview," Sam Dash, OSC/OIC files, p. 2.

201: "The citizen's safety lies in the prosecutor who tempers zeal with human kindness": Televised [and written] Statement of Independent Counsel Robert W. Ray, Friday, January 19, 2001. *Final Report of the Independent Counsel: In Re: Madison Guaranty Savings*

& Loan Association; Regarding Monica Lewinsky and Others, March 6, 2002, p. 1.

202-203: Starr investigation "impartial" or "partisan": The New York Times/CBS news poll, September 25, 1998, question 16.

203: "You think the time, effort, and money spent on the Independent Counsel's investigation has been worth it": Ibid., question 23.

203: "Should Secret Service agents testify": CBS/New York Times Poll, Staff "Keep Secret Service Secret," CBS News, July 21, 1998, https://www.cbsnews.com/news/poll-keep-secret-service-secret/?intcid=CNI-00-10aaa3b

203: "Does testimony interfere with protection?": Ibid.

203: "Evidence was insufficient to prove to a jury beyond a reasonable doubt that either [the] president or Mrs. Clinton knowingly participated in any criminal conduct.": https://abcnews.go.com/Politics/story?id=122883&page=1

"Determined that the evidence was insufficient": Neil A. Lewis, "Whitewater Inquiry Ends; A Lack of Evidence is Cited in Case Involving Clintons," *The New York Times*, September 21, 2000, https://www.nytimes.com/2000/09/21/us/whitewater-inquiry-ends-a-lack-of-evidence-is-cited-in-case-involving-clintons.html

203: "My fundamental concern": Jo Ann Harris phone interview, June 26, 2014.

203-204: "Although some will continue to condemn an acquittal of this President": Laurence Tribe, "And the Winner Is," *The New York Times*, Opinion, February 12, 1999, https://www.nytimes.com/1999/02/12/opinion/and-the-winner-is.html

Epilogue

205-207: "The Secret Service is decidedly nonpartisan and nonpolitical": Excerpts from a speech by Lewis C. Merletti given to the "National Academy (FBI) 'Leadership'" conference in Cleveland, Ohio, March 30, 2000, pp. 3, 4, 6, 7, 8, 9, 12, Merletti files.

207: both parties in Congress concluded that the law had become too susceptible for overreach and allowed the act to lapse: https://www.nytimes.com/2023/01/18/opinion/trump-biden-investigation-special-counsel.html

207: "until Donald Trump": "How Donald Trump Contaminated the Secret Service," by Jeffrey Robinson, *The Daily Beast*, July 23, 2022, https://www.thedailybeast.com/how-donald-trump-contaminated-the-secret-service

"Trump's Secret Service Detail Cheered on The Insurrection": by Gerrard Kaonga, *Newsweek* online magazine, June 29, 2022, https://www.newsweek.com/donald-trump-secret-service-insurrection-carol-leonnig-january-6-capitol-1720235

"Secret Service Ties to Trump Ring Alarm Bells Amid Jan. 6 Revelations": by Darragh Roche, *Newsweek* online magazine, June 30, 2022, https://www.newsweek.com/secret-service-ties-donald-trump-ring-alarm-bells-jan-6-revelations-1720584

Printed in the USA
CPSIA information can be obtained
at www.ICGtesting.com
LVHW011537240923
758828LV00002B/2/J